Luminos is the Open Access monograph
publishing program from UC Press. Luminos
provides a framework for preserving and
reinvigorating monograph publishing for the
future and increases the reach and visibility
of important scholarly work. Titles published
in the UC Press Luminos model are published
with the same high standards for selection, peer
review, production, and marketing as those in our
traditional program. www.luminosoa.org.

The Price of Freedom

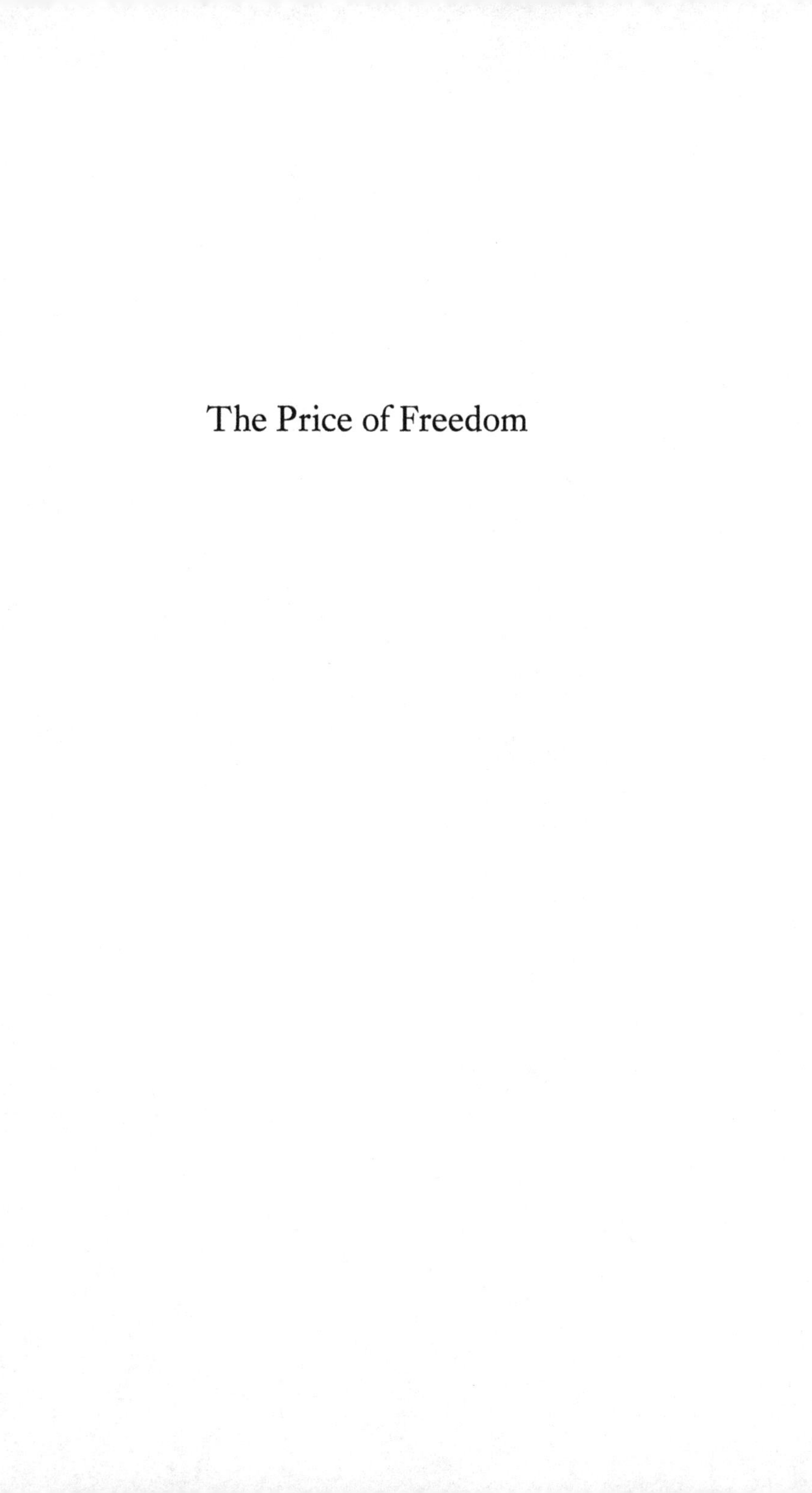

The Price of Freedom

*Criminalization and the
Management of Outsiders
in Germany and the United States*

Michaela Soyer

UNIVERSITY OF CALIFORNIA PRESS

University of California Press
Oakland, California

Suggested citation: Soyer, M. *The Price of Freedom:
Criminalization and the Management of Outsiders in Germany
and the United States.* Oakland: University of California
Press, 2024. DOI: https://doi.org/10.1525/luminos.171

Cataloging-in-Publication Data is on file at the Library
of Congress.

ISBN 978-0-520-39425-4 (pbk. : alk. paper)
ISBN 978-0-520-39426-1 (ebook)

33 32 31 30 29 28 27 26 25 24
10 9 8 7 6 5 4 3 2 1

For Martin Schray

CONTENTS

ACKNOWLEDGMENTS

My first thanks go to the young men and their families in Germany and the United States who shared their stories with me. Without their trust and openness, this book would not have been possible. Maura Roessner has guided *The Price of Freedom* from its first conception to its publication. She is the best editor I could wish for and I am grateful that she continues to help my work find its audience.

The research in Germany became possible after my high school friend Katharina Ebert, now a judge at the Social Welfare Court in Stuttgart, made the relevant introductions to the ministry of justice. Wolfgang Stelly from the Criminological Institute at the University of Tübingen provided crucial support during the data collection process. His work, coauthored with Jürgen Thomas, was essential for my understanding of juvenile justice in Baden-Württemberg.

Being able to write books is a privilege, and I am grateful for my many colleagues, friends, and family who have supported me over the years and made it possible to express my ideas in

writing. Andrea Leverentz, Laura Orrico, and Danielle Raudenbush have been an invaluable part of my academic life over the
past decade. My gratitude also goes to Corey Whichard. Corey
carefully commented on my work and our many conversations
have shaped this book. Bernard Harcourt and his 13/13 semi-
nar series at Columbia University continue to be an intellectual inspiration. Bernard and his students are reminder of why
I wanted to become an academic in the first place. Janina Selzer
has not only worked as a graduate student on the German tran-
scripts, but has also helped me to develop many of the ideas sur-
facing in the book.

My husband Ed Silver and my two children Cordelia and
Rebekka had to put up with my insecurities and frustrations
about writing and research for the past decade. I thank them
for grounding me. My friend Liz Detmeister has served as
a role model for how to manage family and career. She has been a
cheerleader of my work; I am lucky that we met coincidentally
when our children were little, and we remained friends over the
years. Ruky Maria Doerflinger, whom I met when we both trav-
eled to the United States for the first time in 1997 has been more
than a friend. My children are very fortunate to have her in
their lives as an ersatz-aunt.

The Price of Freedom was finalized during a professionally trying time. When I felt anchorless professionally, my friends, my
family, and colleagues at Hunter College were there for me. I
want to thank Gawin Tsai and Neil Ray, who are clearheaded,
kind, and unwaveringly supportive. I am grateful for the support of my colleagues Elke Nicolai and Laura Keating. They
listened and offered strategic, sensible advice. I am also indebted
to Nanda Kalimootoo, who supports the sociology department
at Hunter College administratively. Her open-mindedness,

competence, and kindness made it a lot easier to come to the office when I wanted to hide at home instead. I continue to learn from Mark Halling and his honest perspective. My thanks also go to Jeff London and especially Calvin Smiley, who, as a fellow criminologist, has been an invaluable sounding board.

Introduction

A New Phase for Criminal Justice Reform

After years of public and scholarly debate, the United States' incarceration rates have finally declined significantly. From their height during the early aughts, when 670 people per one hundred thousand were incarcerated, the numbers are now back to the level of 1995, with 556 out of one hundred thousand people in prison. The trend of a steadily increasing prison population has been reversed, but "the Land of the Free" still incarcerates far more people than any comparable European nation (Fair and Walmsley 2021). This outlier status invites international comparisons, but US scholars have mostly looked inward to understand the specific dynamics of crime and incarceration beleaguering the nation since the mid-1980s.[1]

There are many good reasons to shy away from a detailed comparative approach. The United States is unique in its diversity and size. Consequently, the country's political structure is very different from other Western countries (Prasad 2012). In a theoretically rich analysis of the German and American criminal justice systems, Savelsberg (1994) focused on how knowledge production is institutionalized in both countries.

US institutions, he argued, were less bureaucratized and more easily influenced by public sentiments about crime and punishment. German institutions, in contrast, operated more independently from public discourse and did not bend to popular demands as easily.

Today, US journalists, scholars, and nonprofits longingly point to the Nordic countries and Germany as alternatives to the current state of mass incarceration (Turner and Travis 2015; Rudes 2022).[2] The calls for replicating a similar system in the United States fall on fertile ground. Based on a nationally representative survey conducted by the ACLU and Beneson Strategy, a large majority of Americans (92 percent) now believe that reforming the criminal justice system is necessary.[3] High costs of incarceration, combined with high recidivism rates, have led even former supporters of zero tolerance policies to rethink their approach. After only a few days in office President Biden, for example, took executive action and ordered the phasing out of privately operated federal prisons.[4] Netflix shows like *Orange is the New Black* and media personalities like Kim Kardashian have mainstreamed support for criminal justice reform beyond the once small circle of activists and academics.[5]

Given the broad consensus about the need for change in the criminal justice system, Germany can offer insight into what a less retributive system in the United States could look like. A comparison can be especially useful once we bracket Germany's commitment to rehabilitation historically, and scrutinize exclusionary practices that developed beyond official punitive structures. In short: If we want to reform the criminal justice system in the United States, we not only have to consider the kind of policies we would like to implement; we also have to anticipate potential obstacles.

Setting out to understand what it might entail to end mass incarceration, *The Price of Freedom* draws on repeated in-depth interviews with incarcerated young men in Germany and the United States. Comparing the Pennsylvania criminal justice system to the criminal justice system in the southern German state of Baden-Württemberg reveals historical and cultural contingencies that have impacted the development of punitive structures in both countries. As I will show over the course of this book, the seemingly lenient approach to punishment in southern Germany is implemented in tandem with an assumption of cultural homogeneity that would be indefensible in the United States.

Wacquant (2009) and others have argued convincingly that exploding prison populations cannot be understood independently from other social institutions that manage the poor (Fording, Soss, and Schram 2015). In its many more or less punitive iterations (prisons, jails, probation, parole, drug courts, etc.) the criminal justice system has a firm grip on disadvantaged communities across the United States. Building on this argument, *The Price of Freedom* contextualizes the young men's punitive experience in the larger socioeconomic context they grew up in. Comparing educational opportunities, the welfare state, labeling, and discrimination, I show how "outsider status" is constructed and internalized in both countries. Juxtaposing these two very different societies, I argue, allows us to assess why Germany can afford to be less punitive than the United States. Even more importantly, taking a comparative perspective brings into focus what needs to be done to end mass incarceration without increasing strain on segregated communities that are likely to receive the formerly incarcerated.

Building a more humane system of punishment is a complex undertaking in a country as vast and diverse as the United States—especially when reforming the criminal justice system has to go hand in hand with the expansion of social services (Soyer 2018; Sufrin 2017). The kind of safety net that exists in Germany cannot easily be transferred to the United States. The cultural imperative of individualism is incompatible with the idea of an encompassing welfare state that requires financial transparency and cultural assimilation in return for social services (Koopmanns 2010; Barry 2002).

On the other hand, mass incarceration of the poor, disproportionately African American and Latino populations, has shaken the American project of freedom and equality for everyone at its core. Criminal justice reform in the United States therefore needs to balance the different needs of a culturally heterogenous and ideological divided society with offering easily accessible services to those who have been institutionalized for decades. To achieve a more just society, the United States will be required to be more inclusive, more tolerant, and more generous than Western European countries that seem to have built more equal societies, but are still mostly advancing their own ethnically homogenous population.

METHODOLOGY AND FIELDSITES

When I drove through Pennsylvania for the first time in 2013, I was struck by how familiar the landscape felt. The rolling hills, farms at the edge of small towns, and mixed woodlands immediately reminded me of the area I grew up in southern Germany. As I made my way to my new temporary home in State College, I wondered whether the Amish immigrants, who came from southern Germany three hundred years ago, settled here because central Pennsylvania reminded them of the old world they had left behind. The similarity of the landscape is deceptive. In the decades following World War II, the automobile industry turned southern Germany into an economic powerhouse. Large parts of Pennsylvania never recovered from the deindustrialization that devastated once prosperous towns like Allentown or Pittsburgh (Gimple 1999). Unexpected differences hiding behind a familiar façade may be the most adequate way to summarize the cultural and institutional differences between the United States and Germany. *The Price of Freedom* makes use of this particular constellation of likeness and difference to develop a comparative perspective on the processes of marginalization and criminalization in both countries.

As a native German, using Germany as a counterexample to the United States is a natural choice for me. Aside from my personal proclivities, Germany also offers several interesting points of connection. Germany's history has been deeply intertwined with the United States. After World War II, Allied forces under the guidance of the United States allowed Germany to recover and to establish robust democratic structures. For decades US troops were stationed on German soil offering security guarantees against a looming threat from the Soviet Union. Even when the Trump presidency created a rift between both countries, the transatlantic cultural and political exchange remained intact.[6] The persisting cultural difference, in spite of strong political, economic, and cultural connections between the United States and Germany, I argue, offers a unique analytical opportunity. It allows us to conceptualize the potential obstacles the United States might encounter should it emulate a more lenient criminal justice system akin to Germany's.

Data collection for this book proceeded differently at both fieldsites, given the specificity of each criminal justice system. The young men in Pennsylvania faced long prison sentences while the young men in Germany were released within the time frame of this study. As a result, I was able to interview seven of the German respondents again after their release. Depending on their release date, the community interviews in Germany took place between six months to a year after the young men in question had left prison.

At the Pennsylvania fieldsite, I interviewed thirty young men aged between eighteen and twenty-one over the course of three months between April and June 2014. All respondents were incarcerated at the State Correctional Institution (SCI) Pine Grove in central Pennsylvania.[7] They were housed in a unit that is specifically designed for young men who are adjudicated for crimes committed before they turn eighteen.[8] In 2014, approximately three hundred young men were held there. According to the Pennsylvania Juvenile Act, adults remain incarcerated at Pine Grove until they are twenty-two. If they have not finished their sentences by then, they are relocated to adult prisons across the state for the remainder of their sentences.[9]

I recruited participants through an internal communication system that sent a digital call for participation to those people who had a television in their cell. Thirty people agreed to be interviewed and I met with all but one participant three times over the course of three months.[10] A majority of the respondents from Pennsylvania grew up in abject poverty and experienced a high level of childhood trauma. Housing instability, hunger, parental drug use, and being exposed to violence in their homes and neighborhoods were integral parts of the young men's upbringings (Soyer 2018).

The second field site for this project is the juvenile prison located in Adelsheim, a small town in Baden-Württemberg, Germany. In 2017, the German prison housed on average 340 youths aged between fourteen and twenty-four. It is the only juvenile prison left in Baden-Württemberg.[11] Thirteen out of the seventeen German youths who enrolled in this study had a so-called "migration background" (*Migrationshintergrund*), whereas four considered themselves to be ethnically German.[12] The setup of the juvenile prison, as well as the limited number of long-term prisoners, prevented an exact replication of the recruitment strategies utilized in Pennsylvania.

With the support of Wolfgang Stelly, a research associate at the Criminological Institute at the University of Tübingen and member of the Kriminologischer Dienst in Baden-Württemberg, I approached potential respondents individually and presented the research project to them.[13] The young men recruited into the study had a comparable criminal record and similar age range to the Pennsylvania group. Their case files indicated that a majority was not able to complete even the most remedial school work, and several respondents were diagnosed with ADHD. The German young men who participated in the study served between one and five years in prison. Like their counterparts in Pennsylvania, they had been convicted of serious crimes, such as armed robbery, rape, or attempted murder. They were considered to be among the most serious cases in the state.

In addition to interview data, I rely on secondary sources and archival material from the Central Office of the State Justice Administrations for the Investigation of National Socialist Crimes in Ludwigsburg, Baden-Württemberg. This historical perspective traces the development of Germany's criminal justice system post-World War II. The respondents' narratives are contextualized culturally and historically to explore how current constructions of "otherness" relate to Germany's fractured development as a nation (Brubaker 1992).

As is the case for many qualitative studies, this book trades off the number of respondents for in-depth engagement with them. At both sites, respondents were interviewed repeatedly. Owing to time constraints, data collection in Germany took place over the course of three consecutive summers. I observed and interviewed the respondents in different settings—in prison, at group homes, and at home with their families. I was able to document their reentry trajectory, their frustrations, adjustments of expectations, and, in some cases, their disillusionment.

Since most of the young men in Pennsylvania served long sentences, it was not feasible to follow up with them on the outside. However, interviewing the young men repeatedly in prison, and meeting their relatives and friends on the outside, allowed me to build trust and get a deeper understanding of the circumstances of their upbringing. As I have laid out elsewhere, some of the young men disclosed to me for the first time their experience of abuse in the juvenile justice system (Soyer 2018).[14]

The small sample size and the localized data collection do not allow me to draw conclusions that are applicable nationwide in the United States or Germany. In *The Price of Freedom* I take a case-study approach to present theoretical insights into culturally specific processes of the construction of deviance and mass incarceration (Ragin and Becker 1992). The young men shared a variety of narratives that are not representative but indicative of the kind of mechanisms at play in two different judicial systems. Following Max Weber, I consider the two cases "ideal types" that illuminate the contradictions and challenges of two different approaches to social welfare provision and punishment (Weber 1949).

The interpretation of the narratives was a reflexive and hermeneutic exercise. The data were transcribed by research assistants and I coded both data sets using the qualitative word processing software Maxqda. In analyzing the data I referred to my prior work with the Pennsylvania data set and specifically looked for similarities and differences in the categories of childhood trauma, experience of childhood poverty, and provision of social services on the outside. I also added the category of "experience of racism and discrimination" to my analytical tool kit. In contrast to my prior work, this book draws extensively on the experience of discrimination and the young men's identity construction in relation to being "othered." While I deliberately excluded discussions of race and racism in my book *Lost Childhoods*, *The Price of Freedom* utilizes the opportunities inherent in a comparative study to demonstrate how historically contingent constructions of otherness shape young men's understanding of themselves and their social positions.

Again, working in the Weberian tradition, I have focused on the most extreme cases of juvenile crime in both states. The young men I met do not represent the average struggling teenager in both countries. They are extremely disadvantaged, traumatized, and had been institutionalized in various ways multiple times before I met them. Although I make no claims about the generalizability of the data, I do believe that this comparative case study can offer theoretical insights that may broaden the perspective of US scholars, activists, and politicians on the possibilities and challenges of criminal justice reform. Tables 1 and 2 summarize the demographic characteristics of both samples.

TABLE I

American respondents

Name*	Race	Year of birth	Conviction	Sentence†
Alexander	Latino	1993	Theft	2–4 years
Andrew	Mixed	1993	Burglary	2–6 years
Austin	Black	1994	Arson	1–5 years
Blake	Black	1992	Drug manufacture / sale / deliver	1–5 years
Bryan	Black	1993	Carrying firearm w/o license	2–5 years
Connor	Mixed	1994	Robbery	3–10 years
Dylan	Black	1993	Murder 3rd degree	25–50 years
Elijah	Black	1992	Drug manufacture / sale / deliver	3–7 years
Gabriel	Black	1993	Robbery	4–8 years
Henry	White	1994	Theft	2–4 years
Issac	Black	1994	Murder 3rd degree	20–40 years
Jaxon	Black	1994	Robbery	2–8 years
Jeremiah	Black	1993	Aggravated assault	4–8 years
Jesus	Latino	1994	Aggravated harassment	2–4 years
John	Mixed	1994	Robbery	2–3 years
Jordan	Black	1993	Robbery	4–8 years
Joshua	Black	1993	Robbery	2–5 years
Josiah	Black	1993	Burglary	3–6 years
Julian	White	1992	Aggravated assault	4–17 years
Kayden	Black	1994	Aggravated assault	2–4 years
Luke	White	1994	Robbery	3–10 years
Marc	Black	1994	Aggravated assault	9–20 years
Mateo	Latino	1993	Aggravated assault	2–5 years
Miguel	Latino	1992	Robbery	5–10 years
Nate	Asian	1993	Theft of motor vehicles	4–8 years
Oliver	White	1994	Receiving stolen property	9 months–3 years
Robert	White	1993	Sale or transfer of firearms	15–30 years
Samuel	Black	1994	Robbery	2–4 years
Tyler	Black	1992	Robbery	5–12 years
William	White	1994	Aggravated assault	4–8 years

*Names are anonymized.
†Numbers are rounded.

TABLE 2

German respondents

Name*	Parental Country of Origin	Year of Birth	Conviction	Sentence[†]
Carlo	Italy / Togo	1999	Aggravated assault	3 years
Conrad	Germany	1995	Theft, property damage	2 years
Burat	Turkey	1999	Robbery and extortion	4 years
Miro	Kosovo	1996	Aggravated sexual abuse of minors, theft	3 years, 3 months
Thaman	Sri Lanka	~1996	Rape and extortion	3 years
Sahib	India	1996	Attempted murder	6 years
Arslan	Turkey	1994	Attempted murder	5 years, 6 months
Marcel	Germany	1998	Robbery, theft, aggravated assault	2 years, 2 months
Jens	Croatia / Germany	2000	Extortion, aggravated theft	2 years
Martin	Germany	1996	Receiving of stolen property	1 year, 1 month
Achim	Germany	1997	Assault and battery	1 year, 6 months
Johannes	Germany / USA	1997	Assault and battery	1 year, 5 months
Eren	Turkey	1996	Assault, DUI, driving without a license, resisting arrest	3 years, 9 months
Armend	Kosovo	1999	Harassment, theft, trespassing, damage to property	1 year, 6 months
Alexander	Uzbekistan	1997	Aggravated robbery, carrying a firearm	2 years, 9 months
Marko	Roma from Serbia	1995	Assault, DUI, Driving without a License, Resisting Arrest	1 year, 6 months
Adam	Poland	1997	Aggravated assault with a weapon	2 years, 5 months

*Names are anonymized.
[†]Numbers are rounded.

GUNS, VIOLENT CRIME, AND INCARCERATION RATES

An important difference between the two cases is the ready access to guns respondents had in Pennsylvania. The number of people in southern Germany who have a license to own a firearm is negligible in comparison to Pennsylvania, where weapons are for sale at Walmart. According to the Firearms Annual Report by the Pennsylvania State police, among a population of roughly thirteen million people, 1,141,413 firearms were officially purchased or transferred in 2020 alone.[15] In 2022, Baden-Württemberg, with a population of about eleven million, counted about 262,000 registered firearms.[16] As is evident from these numbers, Germany's regulation of gun ownership is much more restrictive. Receiving the permission to own a handgun or rifle is limited to those who hunt or are sport shooters. Owners need to get certified regularly and have to present a psychological evaluation as well. Semiautomatic guns are banned. Not having easy access to guns undoubtedly limited the kind of physical violence the German respondents were able to inflict. They were never involved in shootings or the accidental deaths related to handling loaded weapons. Their neighborhoods were not plagued by gun violence either.

Overall, violent crime is a very rare occurrence in southern Germany. In 2020, Baden-Wuerttemberg had a homicide rate of 2.8 per one hundred thousand people. Pennsylvania in contrast counted 8.5 homicides per one hundred thousand people.[17] On a more local level, Stuttgart, with a population of six hundred thousand—the largest city in Baden-Württemberg—registered four incidents of murder in the first degree in 2021. Seventeen cases were classified as manslaughter. Pittsburgh, the second largest city in Pennsylvania, which is half the size of Stuttgart (approximately three hundred thousand inhabitants) counted fifty-one homicides in 2021.

From a perspective of direct deterrence, the large difference in violent crime rates could explain the discrepancy in incarceration rates between both states. In March 2020 Baden-Württemberg incarcerated 4,537 people in state prisons and held sixty-one people in so-called security confinement, an incarceration rate of approximately 41.2 per one hundred thousand people. (Staatistisches Landesamt 2020).[18] During the same month, Pennsylvania's state prison population was 44,230, which equals an incarceration rate of about 340 per one hundred thousand people. The state government in Pennsylvania had a homicide rate that was about three times the size of Baden-Württemberg with an incarceration rate that was approximately 8.25 higher than in southern Germany. The large variance in incarceration and crime rates raises the question of how comparable the two field sites actually are. I maintain that the numerical differences can make a comparative case study more compelling. Understanding how punishment, violence and incarceration relates to the historical and cultural idiosyncrasies of both societies, points to the challenges of reforming the US criminal justice system.

Given the analytical goals of this book, I decided to bracket the question of why the United States has higher crime rates than other comparable Western nations. This decision does not imply that I consider the differences in violent crime to be irrelevant. On the contrary, they deserve to be investigated in depth and they go beyond the scope of this book.[19] The objective of *The Price of Freedom* is not to establish causal mechanisms between violent crime and incarceration rates. On the contrary, the following chapters investigate the meaning of punishment not just as a retributive or deterrent tool of governance but as a form of meaning making and boundary maintenance (Erickson 2004; Durkheim 1960). The following section provides a brief overview of the main arguments and a summary of the different chapters.

CHAPTER 1. HOMOGENEITY, PUNISHMENT, AND THE WELFARE STATE

Chapter 1 introduces the theoretical framework guiding the data analysis. *The Price of Freedom* draws on Durkheim's writings on punishment in *The Division of Labor in Society* (1960). Durkheim proposes that focusing on how societies sanction behavior reveals their general organizing principle (1960, 128). Highly developed and heterogenous societies that operate according to the principles of "organic solidarity" are more tolerant of differences and therefore less punitive (1960, 112f). Homogenous and less-developed communities that are organized according to mechanical solidarity punish harshly. Difference is perceived as a threat to their core functioning (1960, 108).

A comparison of Germany and the United States adds to these classic assertions in unexpected ways. Germany has a seemingly lenient punishment regime that is comparable to the Nordic countries. Like those countries, Germany is a fairly homogenous society less willing to tolerate expressions of different ethnic identities (Plamper 2019; Panreck and Brinkmann 2019; Koopmans 2010; Joppke 1999). The United States, on the other hand, is more flexible when it comes to accommodating different ethnic communities. Visible difference is accepted as long as individuals operate effectively within the logic of capitalist society (Merton 1938; Messner and Rosenfeld 2007). Punitive structures in the United States therefore tend to have the greatest impact on those who have fallen through cracks of the hypercapitalist economic system.

Investigating these tensions, chapter 1 uses Durkheim's theoretical construct to explore the differences between the punitive traditions in both countries. Durkheim's assumptions about the connections between punishment and social solidarity provide a blueprint for exploring how punishment connects to general social, political, and economic practices in the respective countries. While Durkheim's theoretical apparatus can seem reductive, its simplicity clarifies how both countries have historically managed and punished "outsiders." Contradicting the widespread assumption of US scholars that Western European countries like Sweden, Finland, or Germany could be a model for more humane punishment in the United States, this chapter shows that a seemingly more lenient system of punishment does not necessarily imply a more tolerant and inclusive society.

CHAPTER 2. THE UNCERTAINTY OF BELONGING: NARRATIVES OF DIFFERENCE AND EXCLUSION IN GERMANY AND THE UNITED STATES

Chapter 2 focuses on how social constructions of race and citizenship have shaped the respondents' identity in both locations. To illustrate how the young men narrativize their experience, this chapter compares multiple cases of German-Turkish and German-Russian young men with Latino and African American respondents from the United States. Since 1999, the reform of the German citizenship law has offered children of immigrant parents a pathway to citizenship. This official movement from ius saguinis to ius soli nevertheless maintains firm boundaries for those deemed undeserving of citizenship (Anil 2007). Even children who are able to become German citizens are not considered part of the German community. The German census defines second- and even third-generation immigrants as people living in Germany with a "migration background" in perpetuity.

The US respondents do not have to worry about their status as US citizens. Their exclusion manifests economically as they are subject to institutional racism and segregation (Sharkey 2013; Alexander 2010; Pattillo 1999; Massey and Denton 1994). As a result, the narratives of the young men reflect security in their American identity even though their life-course history testifies to the marginalization they have suffered.

Taking cultural and structural differences seriously, chapter 2 sheds light on the complexity of US society in comparison to a homogenous country like Germany. To this day, Germany defines belonging in terms of ethnicity that is inherited across generations. As the legacy of the atrocities committed during the Third Reich recede into the background, demands for harsher punishments, especially for immigrants and their children, have become more socially acceptable (Walter 2003). The influx of refugees has given rise to an anti-immigrant political rhetoric. The so-called *Alternative für Deutschland* (AfD), a party explicitly running on a law-and-order, anti-immigrant platform has been elected by a large margin to the state parliament in Baden-Württemberg. Those who are not ethnically German never truly belong (Yurdakul and Korteweg 2013; Korteweg and Yurdakul 2014). Understanding the explicit and implicit exclusionary mechanism prevalent in southern German society challenges the country's progressive image, often cited as a counterexample to the racist system of mass incarceration in the United States (Alexander 2010).[20]

CHAPTER 3. "HERE, I GET THREE MEALS A DAY": SEGREGATION AND THE RELATIVE EXPERIENCE OF POVERTY

The different narratives presented in this chapter expose the relativity of suffering and poverty. Poverty and incarceration in both field sites were experienced in relation to the living standard of the surrounding environment (Hochschild 1989). German respondents initially perceived their outsider status more intensely than the American sample did. They had been confronted with the lifestyle of the majority white middle class on a daily basis before they were sent to prison. While punitive measures were comparatively mild, the young men understood very well that incarceration entrenched their marginalization. American respondents, in contrast, had lived in segregated, poverty-stricken neighborhoods before they were sent to prison. The American sample was so far removed from middle- and upper-middle-class life, that the young men only conceptualized the full scope their disadvantage after the fact (Shedd 2015).

The narratives of the US respondents also revealed that extreme poverty and segregation in the United States undermine the principle of "less eligibility" (Rusche and Kirchheimer 2003).

The "upper limit," the living standard of the poorest worker on the outside, is now so low that prisons—following the constitutional mandate of preventing "cruel and unusual punishment"—cannot keep pace (Bonnet 2019). For the young men in the United States, life on the outside had reached such desperate proportions that being incarcerated elevated their living conditions. In prison they were able to access at least minimal social services that had been out of reach on the outside (Soyer 2018; Sufrin 2017).

CHAPTER 4. RETRIBUTION AND DOMINATION: LIVING THROUGH PUNISHMENT IN GERMANY AND THE UNITED STATES

Chapter 4 develops a comparative historical perspective on the different punitive mechanisms applied in southern Germany and Pennsylvania. Contextualizing the narratives of the young men historically and culturally illustrates that lenient punishment in Germany is a fairly new development that needs to be understood in terms of Germany's unique path of nation-building and the catastrophe of World War II. Secondly, this chapter argues that criminal justice in Baden-Württemberg has to be analyzed in tandem with the welfare state. Through their parents' entanglement with the welfare state, the young men in Germany had been integrated in the disciplinary apparatus of welfare governance from early childhood on. Unlike their American counterparts, the German respondents did not report committing crimes out of desperation. Likewise, their punishment was lighter than the punitive experience of the American sample. In aggregate, however, they were subject to disciplinary mechanisms and homogenizing pressures long before they entered prison.

Germany's punishment regime is juxtaposed with the US system of mass incarceration. Retracing the paradox of a society that is at once committed to free market economy while maintaining an inhumane and costly system of mass incarceration, this chapter draws on work by Loïc Wacquant (2009) and others (Garland 2002; Edin and Shaefer 2015; Sufrin 2017). Synthesizing these prior contributions, chapter 3) argues that the carceral state in the United States has haphazardly filled the void of a dismantled welfare system (Soyer 2018). Contradicting PRWORA's (Personal Responsibility and Work Opportunity Act) intentions to minimize state intervention and increase participation in the workforce, mass incarceration has removed a significant number of people from the labor market. Managing a population with decade-long sentences, prisons have inadvertently resorted to the kind of permanent and more extreme government maintenance the welfare reform was supposed to counteract.

CHAPTER 5. "I WANNA BE SOMEBODY": EDUCATION AND UPWARD MOBILITY IN GERMANY AND THE UNITED STATES

This chapter focuses on how education in Germany and the United States has shaped the respondents' ideas about their opportunities and ability to achieve their goal of living a middle -class life. Narratives of the young men are scaffolded by a structural analysis of both educational systems.

Germany has a long tradition of a dual educational system that offers less academically inclined teenagers the opportunity to receive formal training in a trade (i.e., as a mechanic, hairdresser, plumber, and so on). Decisions about a child's future are made in fourth grade, when students, aged nine or ten, are either sent to vocational schools or academic high schools. Although it is possible to switch between tracks, moving from the vocational school system to the academic high school system remains the exception (Bernhard 2017). To enter a German university, students have to pass the *Abitur,* thereby obtaining a degree that is roughly equivalent to the American high school diploma or the British A-levels. Those who come from immigrant families are less likely to achieve this milestone than children of native German families (Baumert, Maaz, and Trautwein 2010; Diehl and Granato 2018). While teenagers who did not finish high school have many opportunities to find gainful employment, their earning potential and upward mobility are curtailed (Aybek 2008).

Similar to Germany, minorities in the United States are disadvantaged when it comes to accessing high-quality education. African American and Latino students are more likely to attend underfunded schools in high-crime neighborhoods with low graduation rates (Shedd 2015). High school dropouts in the United States are more likely to be unemployed than high school graduates. If they find work, they tend to get paid lower salaries than those who finished their high school diploma (McCaul et al. 1992; McFarland, Rathbun, and Holmes 2019).

The difference between both samples manifests itself in the young men's hopes and dreams for their future. In the absence of institutional pathways to success, several American participants subscribed to a vague idea of entrepreneurship. This allowed them to maintain the illusion of agency while they were in a holding pattern, waiting to be transferred to another institution (Soyer 2016). German participants who were unable to secure an apprenticeship focused on a specific skill—for example, forklift driving.

The German young men had already leveled their expectations, while the young men at SCI Pine Grove seemed to hold out hope that the "American Dream" of upward mobility and property ownership could still become a reality for them (Soyer 2016). In the end, optimism was difficult to sustain for both samples. Even as they expressed hope for a better future, past experience had taught them how difficult it would be for them to live successful and engaged lives.

SUMMARY

Comparing two societies and their approaches to managing difference, *The Price of Freedom* argues that both countries can learn from each other as they conceptualize a more equal and tolerant future. Despite their experience of racism and segregation, Latino and African American respondents are secure in their identity as Americans—even as American society fails to deliver on its promise of equality and opportunity. Germany, in contrast, does not promise upward mobility and unlimited opportunities to its minority populations. Instead, the country offers social citizenship for everyone, thereby preventing the abject poverty that haunted the American sample. At the same time, the narratives of the German young men show that being entangled in the welfare state comes at a cost as well. Growing up surrounded by middle-class and upper-middle-class prosperity, the respondents knew that they had to live on what the government had allocated to their families, while the white German majority thrived around them.

The southern German sample felt restricted in abstract terms, while the confinement of young men in Pennsylvania was a concrete experience. Those who served long sentences had to learn how to cope with the psychological burden of knowing that they would be spending most of their young adulthood in prison (Soyer 2018). For others with shorter sentences, reentry into the community brought the fear of economic uncertainty. They expected minimal government support and had no clear path to achieving even modest goals, such as stable employment (Soyer 2016). Expanding the social welfare net may ease significant suffering in the United States, while expanding the notion of citizenship and belonging would be transformative for those that have been labeled outsiders in Germany for generations.

In the same manner, the German apprentice system could be a model for the United States, regardless of the early leveling the German educational system seems to promote. Almost paradoxically, while someone who has been recently released from prison in the United States may struggle to find gainful employment, his or her opportunities to obtain a four-year college degree are better than they are for a young person in Germany who has been tracked into vocational training. Obtaining a GED offers a clear path to community college and eventually a four-year degree. While the community college pathway is shaped by resource scarcity, community colleges open doors to higher education for economically disadvantaged students of color (Goldrick-Rab 2010). As I will show over the course of this book, both societies have their blind spots, as well as racial and social divisions, which are taken for granted and have not been addressed adequately.

CHAPTER ONE

Homogeneity, Punishment, and the Welfare State

> My plan in coming here was to displace by some knowledge, the legend of the United States that one learns abroad. That this is a crime ridden, gang ridden country is the German legend.
>
> Uwe Johnson, author of *Anniversaries, New York Times,* April 23, 1967

Around Christmas 2021, I had the first conversation in more than two decades with my aunt. My father's younger sister had left southern Germany with her GI husband to move to Texas sixty years ago. At seventy-seven she was suffering from the early stages of dementia. As she was beginning to lose her short-term memory, she sought to reconnect with her German roots. When I spoke to her on the phone, she told me that she wished she could go back to Germany: "When I was young," she said, "I didn't know that America was that far away."

I cannot begin to conceptualize how strange Texas must have seemed to my aunt, who did not speak any English when she arrived there in the early 1960s. When I came to Chicago in 2006, I knew English well. I had grown up around American pop culture and I was there to go to graduate school, not to escape the ruins of World War II. In the four decades between my aunt's and my own arrival, the United States and Germany have become culturally and politically more similar to each other. Nevertheless, even if Berlin and New York City have turned into global cities (Sassen 1991), both Germany and the United States retain historically specific and culturally contingent social and economic structures.

Historical contingencies and competing hypotheses about nation-building turn the comparative analysis of punitive structures in Germany and the United States into a daunting exercise. Joachim Savelsberg is one of the few social theorists whose work takes on the idiosyncratic social and institutional practices that have shaped criminal justice policies in both countries. Savelsberg (1994) seeks to understand why Germany became less punitive than the United States, even though crime rates increased in both countries. For Savelsberg the answer to this empirical puzzle is partly a cultural one: The United States and Germany adhere to very different ideas about the individual and the individual's role in society. These ideological presumptions inadvertently generate specific interpretations of the cause and prevention of criminal behavior.

Comparing Germany and the United States on multiple social dimensions (i.e., the public sphere, academia, the political sector, the institutionalization of domination, social structure, and conflict), he concludes that public discourse translates into policy much more directly in the United States than in Germany (924–925). The jury trial, for example, sets the stage for communal judgment. In contrast to Germany, US district attorneys are subject to an electoral process. Roughly equivalent government officials in Germany are appointed as civil servants whose positions are secured for life (ibid.).[1] Savelsberg also understands political decision-making in Germany to be beholden to the Weberian logic of "legal domination." Germany's bureaucratic structure, he argues, prevents policies that respond to soaring crime rates with harsher sentencing.

Like Savelsberg, James Q. Whitman (2001) believes that a "strong state" has protected Germany and France from becoming as punitive as the United States during the last decade of the twentieth century. According to Whitman, bureaucracies in both countries have enabled an individualistic approach to punishment that leaves room for "mercy" (14). He also argues that Germany and France fought against differential treatment of the upper classes for centuries. Germany and France, he writes, used to punish the wealthy more humanely than the lower classes. As both countries have sought to flatten social hierarchies, they have expanded "soft" punishment to everyone (11).

Where Savelsberg focuses his analysis on contemporary Germany, Whitman takes a historical perspective. Attempting to fit the years between 1933 and 1945 into his path-dependent analysis, he maintains that the Nazi regime continued to individualize punishment. Whitman insists that the criminal justice system during the Third Reich aspired to reintegrate prisoners incarcerated for conventional crimes as members of the German "Volk"—even if it did so while exercising harsh forms of punishment (141).

German historians who have studied "career criminals" as "forgotten victims" of the Nazis present a different perspective. In 1933, the Nazi regime introduced "security confinement" into the repertoire of sentencing. The concept has survived Germany's defeat at the hands of the Allies in 1945. To this day, "security confinement" presupposes that certain offenders are incorrigible and may have to be held indefinitely. During the Nazi dictatorship security confinement was also a tool to manage the "biological stock" of the German people. Being incarcerated without a release date prevented "inferior" individuals from marrying and having children (Lieske 2016, 53–54).

Savelsberg and Whitman both argue that a detached bureaucracy insulates Germany from giving into popular demands for harsher forms of punishment for criminals. Defining German bureaucracy and its tradition to exercise power "sine ira et studio" (Weber 1978) as a bulwark against harsher punitive politics becomes more ambivalent once we include the years between 1933 and 1945 in our analysis. In light of the Nazi atrocities, social theorists, historians, and philosophers have famously argued the exact opposite: the German bureaucratic machine played a crucial part in the execution of the "Final Solution." Without a state apparatus able and willing to execute orders without moral concern, the finality and scale of the Holocaust could not have been accomplished (Adorno and Horkheimer 1944; Hilberg 1999; Arendt 1963; Bauman 1989).

The institutional and individual continuity in Germany after World War II is widely documented as well. The postwar German criminal justice system, in particular, was inevitably intertwined with the institutions and personnel of the Third Reich (Hölzl 2002, 2019). Nevertheless, implementing a more humane criminal justice system was politically inevitable. The "new" Germany needed to demonstrate to the Allied powers that it had truly changed. The bureaucratic apparatus followed suit and reoriented itself quickly to the new political reality (Frei 2014; Aust 1985).

THE MAKING OF A LENIENT CRIMINAL
JUSTICE SYSTEM

Like Savelsberg and Whitman, I also believe that structural-functionalist theories of punishment fail to grapple with the complexity of cultural contingencies. However, I maintain that Durkheim's concept of punishment as strengthening "collective conscience" provides useful analytical leverage when we juxtapose homogenous versus heterogenous societies. According to Durkheim (1964), homogeneity forms the basis of mechanical solidarity—a solidarity of likeness (70). In *The Division of Labor in Society*, Durkheim connected the type of solidarity prevalent in a society to the kind of punishment a community gravitates toward. For Durkheim, "punishment" is a form of boundary maintenance, allowing the group to reiterate and solidify their norms and values. Consequently, a behavioral choice is deemed "criminal" if it violates the "collective conscience." As he put it, "Crime brings together upright consciences and concentrates them" (102).

Durkheim also believed that societies connected through a "solidarity of likeness" respond repressively to violations of their "collective conscience." Any act that questions the normative assumptions of such a group threatens the group's existence and cannot be tolerated. Highly developed and heterogeneous societies, by contrast, operate according to the principles of "organic solidarity." Those societies are connected through the shared purpose of the division of labor and are supposed to be more tolerant of differences and therefore less punitive (1964, 112–13).

When Durkheim developed his dichotomy between "organic" and "mechanic solidarity," he juxtaposed what he saw as "primitive" social groups with the industrializing societies of Western

Europe. Durkheim's colonialist fascinations may not have aged well, but the *Division of Labor* can still provide a useful framework for comparative analysis. For example, both the United States and Germany operate according to the rules of global, advanced capitalism. The societies of both countries should follow principles of organic solidarity and their respective punitive processes should be conciliatory rather than retributive. For obvious reasons, Durkheim's model fits neither the United States nor Germany particularly well. With around six hundred people incarcerated per one hundred thousand inhabitants, the United States has famously become the country with the highest incarceration rate in the world (Carson 2020). In comparison, Germany's incarceration rate is much smaller and hovers at 76.2 people per one hundred thousand inhabitants (SPACE 2016). Paradoxically, Germany's low incarceration rates don't imply a more tolerant society. Through its many iterations, Germany has continued to define itself as a *Gemeinschaft*, systematically excluding immigrants from the *Volk* (Tönnies, 1957; see also chapter 2). Even though German society tends to be connected by a "solidarity of likeness," its justice system seems to be far less punitive than the United States.

The tension between "theory" and complex "praxis" comes even more into focus when we look at the historical circumstances engulfing Germany during and after World War II. Germany's commitment to the rehabilitative ideal is a fairly recent development—especially when we include the former GDR. Until 1989, the GDR government incarcerated political prisoners under inhumane conditions. In the infamous Stasi prison "Bautzen II" in Saxony, solitary confinement was the norm. Prisoners were referred to by their numbers not their names (Klewin and Wenzel 2003). During the Ninth Congress of the Communist Party in 1972, the Western German magazine *Der Spiegel* quoted Erich Seitz, then attorney general of the GDR, who stated that the government should create an "unforgiving atmosphere" (*Atmosphäre der Unversöhnlichkeit*) and use "unremittingly harsh measures" (*unveränderte Strenge*) against all criminal elements. He was particularly concerned, though, with "enemies of the current order." Those should be treated without forbearance (*ohne Nachsicht*).[2]

The blatant human rights violations of the GDR allowed the Federal Republic to position itself more effectively as a changed country that had put the atrocities of World War II behind itself. Under the tutelage of the United States, Western Germany had embraced the doctrine of protecting "human dignity" as the ultimate principle of governance and legal proceedings in 1949. Germany's newly found commitment to "human dignity" stood in contrast to the uncompromising, self-destructive inhumanity of the Third Reich. As Ian Kershaw described in his account of the Reich's final months, local police forces continued to execute "traitors," even with American tanks in sight (2011).

Between 1933 and 1945, so-called "special courts" executed more than 5,600 people for political crimes. During the same time frame, military courts executed more than thirty thousand people for desertion, refusal to serve, or undermining military goals (Tuchel 2019).[3] In 1949, when the new parameters of the German constitution were drafted, a majority of Germans (74 percent) still wanted to retain the death penalty as a mode of punishment.[4] In the end, an unlikely coalition across party lines, including communists and right-wing nationalists, voted in favor of Article 102,[5] thereby abolishing the death penalty (see the survey of the demographic institute in Allensbach cited in Schlieben 2019; von Kittlich 2019).[6] Curiously, and some historians argue intentionally, the earliest beneficiaries of Article 102 (then 103), were Nazi henchmen, put on trial by the German government during the 1950s and 1960s (Evans 1997).[7]

In 1958, the German government decided to concentrate the investigation of Nazi crimes in a single government institution—the "Central Office of the State Justice Administrations for the Investigation of National Socialist Crimes" in Ludwigsburg, Baden-Württemberg. The investigators in Ludwigsburg had to rely on local district attorney offices to follow up on leads and to send information back to them. The reluctance of the bureaucratic machine to investigate Germans implicated in the Nazi war crimes, is on full display in the case of former SS-Oberscharführer, Wilhelm Boger.

Even in a place as merciless as Auschwitz, Boger was known for his brutality. Prisoners referred to him simply as "Der Tod" (Death) and he was eventually sentenced to life in prison during the Frankfurt Auschwitz trials in 1963 (Pendas 2010). A skilled torturer, Boger had been in charge of collecting intelligence among Auschwitz prisoners to prevent a potential uprising. After Germany's defeat, Boger was captured by US forces, who planned to hand him over to Polish authorities, but he managed to escape during his transport to Poland. After living for several years under an assumed identity, Boger eventually returned to his home state, Baden-Württemberg. There he felt comfortable enough to use his real name again, and he settled down with his family in the small village of Hemmingen (Klee 2013).

Had it not been for the "career criminal" and notorious troublemaker Adolf Rögner, Boger would likely have never been held responsible for his crimes. Born in 1904, Adolf Rögner had been incarcerated repeatedly for fraud during the Weimar Republic and the Third Reich. Deemed incorrigible, he was first sent to the concentration camp in Dachau and later transferred to Auschwitz, where he encountered Boger. After the war, Rögner recidivated and was again sentenced to prison for fraud. As the German postwar "economic miracle" took off without him, he kept track of the many former Auschwitz guards that had gotten away. Rögner not only knew that Boger had escaped; he had also learned that the former SS sergeant did not hide anymore. In 1958, Rögner, then incarcerated at a prison in Baden-Württemberg, sent a letter to the district attorney's office in Stuttgart reporting the whereabouts of a potential war criminal. The district attorney's office confirmed that Boger existed and indeed lived in a small town. Then the investigation fizzled. The district attorney's office slow-walked further scrutiny of Boger's past until a more prominent and less ambiguous Auschwitz survivor, Hermann Langbein, intervened. As the head of the Auschwitz Committee,[8] he called a press conference, revealed Boger's place of residence, and pointed to the district attorney's inaction. Following the public attention that was drawn to the matter, Boger was eventually arrested and interrogated in October 1958—seven months after Rögner had sent his initial letter.[9]

Boger was one of six defendants sentenced to life in prison during the Auschwitz trials. The majority of his codefendants were treated more leniently. Former SS sergeant Hans Stark, another guard Rögner identified, had served in Auschwitz when was nineteen years old. Under the new laws of the Federal Republic, he was considered a minor at the time he had committed his crimes and had to be tried as a juvenile.[10] Stark admitted in court to gassing 250 Jews and participating in the shooting of Soviet prisoners of war. One witness, whose father was among Stark's victims, testified that Stark had ordered a Jewish prisoner to chase fellow inmates into a ditch filled with water. They were supposed to be drowned there. The inmate, who had carried out Stark's orders at gunpoint, started screaming. Stark shot him dead.[11]

Sentenced under German juvenile law, Stark was handed a ten-year prison sentence. After serving three years, he was released in 1968. An obituary commissioned by his former employer and published in the *Darmstädter Echo* in 1991 testified to his seamless reintegration. After his release, he worked for the chemical company Merck until his retirement in 1983. The obituary also praised his personality and his expertise in crop protection. In the end, Stark, who had killed hundreds of Jews, spent significantly less time incarcerated than Adolf Rögner a nonviolent offender, whose mental and physical health had been severely impacted by his experiences in Dachau and Auschwitz.[12]

Germany's treatment of Nazi perpetrators was in line with the United States' pragmatic approach to denazification that emerged after the Nuremberg trials. Hoping to utilize Western Germany as an ally against Russia, the US government was compelled to fast-track rehabilitation of second- or third-tier Nazi officials. Balancing continuity and necessary political change, the United States, Great Britain, and France still sought to prevent a "re-nazification" of Germany (Rigoll 2017). The establishment of a more humane judicial system, under the auspice of the Western Allies, was supposed to be safeguard against a potential resurgence of fascism.

Meanwhile, the German people, united by the sins and trauma of World War II, yearned for collective and individual redemption (Jähner 2019). Subordinating the execution of justice to the protection of human dignity solved two problems at once: It underscored Germany's presentation as a "reformed" country, while limiting serious punishment of Nazi war criminals.[13]

It became apparent quickly that the benefits of rehabilitation and humane punishment were not extended equally across the political spectrum. Dating back to the Weimar Republic, the German judiciary had always been more tolerant of violence from the Right than the Left (Gumbel 2012). A case in point was the willingness and capacity of the German government to expand executive powers and increase the reach of law enforcement when terrorists from the Left threatened the status quo of the Federal Republic. During the 1970s, the Red Army Faction (RAF), an outgrowth of the student movement, assassinated prominent industrialists and politicians. Under Chancellor Helmut Schmidt, the government enacted new anti-terrorism laws and established investigative tactics akin to racial profiling to identify potential RAF supporters.[14] Until today, German left-leaning intellectuals wonder whether the German justice system turns "a blind eye to right-wing extremism."[15]

In terms of Durkheim's theory, Germany's example indicates that mechanical solidarity and a lenient criminal justice system can coexist when those who have committed crimes represent—at least in part—the norms and values of the majority. During the 1970s, when terrorism from the Left posed a real threat to the political and economic establishment, the government bureaucracy responded with astonishing flexibility and speed (Rigoll 2013).[16] Similarly, as Germany has become more diverse, the country's rehabilitative approach to punishment has been questioned by the political Right (see chapter 2). Although sentencing has remained comparatively lenient, exclusion and labeling manifest in subtle but consequential ways for those who are not ethnically German (Spindler 2011). The young men I interviewed were acutely aware of their outsider status, their lack of belonging, and their limited chances of upward mobility.

"SUPERPREDATORS" AND THE "FREE MARKET"

In the United States, punitive processes have swung back and forth like a pendulum between retribution and rehabilitation. During the 1960s, rehabilitation and reintegration were at the forefront of penal policies (Rubin 2019; Garland 2001). The most recent punitive turn has been documented extensively. The war on drugs, the fear of "superpredators" (DiIulio 1995), and opportunistic neoliberal governance set off a twofold development: the destruction of the welfare state and the expansion of the criminal justice system (Wacquant 2009). As an unintended consequence of these institutional changes, the criminal justice system has taken over functions of the welfare state and has become a major provider of social services for the poor (Haney 2010; Sufrin 2017). My first book, *A Dream Denied* (2016), elaborates on this phenomenon in great depth. Analyzing the pathways of young men through two juvenile justice systems in Boston and Chicago showed that punishment and welfare provision were entangled in unfortunate ways. The young men I interviewed had to be "punished"—sent to detention center or juvenile prison—to receive comprehensive treatment of mental health challenges or educational support. As I wrote in 2016, "The judicial system was often the only governmental organization providing even nominal support for inner-city children and their families. Without their probation officers, the teenagers were at greater risk of slipping through the cracks of an underfunded social welfare system" (3). The exact causes of exploding prison population in the mid-1990s are still up for debate (Paff 2017). It is indisputable, though, that mass incarceration has done disproportionate damage to already marginalized African American and Latino families (Western 2006; Clear 2007;

Alexander 2010; Western and Pettit 2010; Wakefield and Wildemann 2013; Lee and Wildemann 2021).

Using Durkheim's assumptions as a heuristic tool reveals the absurdity the United States confront today: the country should be a society held together by "organic solidarity." The direct and indirect economic implications of incarcerating a significant amount of the population contradict American ideals such as the "free market economy," "small government," and "meritocracy."

As a structural functionalist, Durkheim did not have a particularly fine-grained concept of the different motivations that drive social action. He believed that individual motivations are inevitably linked to universal, collective goals (106). His theory therefore fails to capture the complexity of modern societies in which different institutional contexts are aligned with different types of social action. Collaboration in the market place, for example, is an instrumental rational act with the goal of maximizing one's utility (Weber 1978). Solidarity established in a market place may not require empathetic, intersubjective role-taking (Mead 1967; Habermas 1985). The different factions may work together for the shared goal of profit, but they are unlikely to develop a "collective conscience" that overcomes gender, race, and class divisions.

For example, a white male manager does not have to actively "collaborate" with his female African American administrative assistant. He has power over her (Blau 1986), the kind of power that forces her to collaborate with him. This hypothetical "boss" may treat his employee with courtesy, but in the end their relationship is asymmetrical. Even if we consider a relationship among equals, the tolerance we can muster for a productive colleague that looks different, worships differently, and speaks with an accent may fade away quickly once this person does not fulfill a "useful" function for us anymore.

While the United States may cease to be a majority white country in the near future, the ethnic and racial divisions within it persist. Intermarriage rates remain low, segregation continues to be high, and the white population still holds the majority of wealth and power. In a way that is very different from the situation in Germany, those who are poor, the "misfits" and "outsiders," not only look very different, they also embody different norms and values than the disproportionality white upper-middle-class center of power. Punishing those "outsiders" harshly makes sense psychologically because it justifies the current status quo without any economic costs for the higher echelons of American society.

Turning Durkheim's logic around, I argue that the United States punishes differently than Germany because it is a more heterogenous country. Being held together by the instrumental rational logic of the market place has made the United States more tolerant of different lifestyles, norms, and values as long as people are actively contributing to the nation's surplus value (Merton 1938). At the same time, US society is much less tolerant than Germany's "community" of those who are not participating in the labor market to maximize their economic gain.

THE WELFARE STATE

Punishment in both countries cannot be fully understood without an investigation of its ancillary—the welfare state. Welfare services and punishment cover overlapping populations and utilize similar tactics to manage the marginalized. The Quakers who founded Eastern State Penitentiary saw themselves as reformers whose strategies were supposed to convert "deviants" into productive members of society (Rothman 2008). Likewise, the juvenile justice system was established as an attempt to develop an alternative to the adult criminal justice system to "uplift youth" rather than punishing them (Mack 1909). Under the guise of rehabilitation, welfare provisions have always remained a staple of modern punishment even during the era of mass incarceration (Phelps 2011). Today's abolitionists also envision a system in which punishment is replaced with comprehensive social services for vulnerable populations (Davis 2003).

Replacing punishment with welfare services addresses the immediate suffering abject poverty causes (Soyer 2018). At the same time, welfare measures—like punishment—are designed to discipline their constituency. The modern welfare state is supposed to provide a temporary stopgap that allows recipients to restore their contribution to economic production. But if participation in the workforce is unfeasible, access to social services appeases the poor, prevents collective organization, and secures their docility (Plath 1977; Foucault 1975; Piven and Cloward 1993; Soss, Fording, and Schram 2015). Even measures directed at upper-middle-class clients incentivize compliance. For example, the interest free German student loan program rewards fast repayment with partial debt cancellation.[17]

Those who rely on welfare to meet their basic needs have to operate within narrow parameters. The US Supplemental Nutrition Assistance Program (SNAP) limits items that can be purchased with government funds. In addition to liquor and cigarettes, prepared meals, pet foods or cleaning supplies are ineligible purchases under the SNAP program as well.[18] In order to receive Section 8 housing assistance, tenants, in renting their apartments, have to meet strict conditions.[19]

Inevitably, public discourse surrounding welfare reform centers on limiting access to those who are "truly" deserving of help, rather than wasting resources on people who are simply "too lazy" to enter the workforce. In the United States, the rhetoric about the abuse of welfare privileges has centered on stereotypical depictions of minorities, propagating, most infamously, the myth of the African American "welfare queen."[20] Calls for dismantling welfare in the United States became synonymous with cutting off support for "promiscuous" inner-city minority women, who supposedly used government checks to support their lavish spending. The welfare reform in 1995 turned welfare into workfare. Provisions like the Earned Income Tax credit were supposed to encourage labor force participation, and the time limits put on Temporary Assistant for Needy Families (TANF) effectively prevented anyone but the most desperate form applying (Edin and Shaefer 2015).

In Germany the welfare state has never been completely dismantled. Even limited attempts to do so were met with extensive public outrage (Rucht and Yang 2004). Those pushing for reform believed that generous and unlimited unemployment benefits disincentivized finding work. In contrast to the United States, the debate in Germany lacked a racial undertone. Now, it may have been the case that twenty years ago, Germans still shied away from an open discourse about race and eligibility. More likely, however, race was irrelevant because those deemed least eligible—refugees—are blocked from legal employment and never benefited from the generous unemployment benefits that were in place prior to 2005.

When it comes to long-term unemployment, ethnic Germans have been the main beneficiaries of unemployment insurance. According to the ministry of labor, almost 60 percent of those who struggled with long-term unemployment were ethnically German (Fritz, Lüdeke, and Wolff 2020).

The policy changes, referred to as Hartz IV reforms, took effect in 2005 and undeniably strengthened the welfare bureaucracy's punitive abilities with regard to citizens. While Germany has retained unlimited welfare benefits, the state now distinguishes between those who are temporarily unemployed, those who are likely to reenter the workforce, and those who struggle with long-term unemployment. Currently, benefits are divided into several different, rather complex, stages of support: "Unemployment I" (Arbeitslosengeld I) payments cover approximately 60 percent of your final paycheck. Payments also depend on the length of prior employment. Those who suffer from prolonged unemployment receive "Unemployment II" (Arbeitslosengeld II). People too old or otherwise unable to work a minimum of three hours daily are eligible for social welfare payments (*Sozialgeld*). Overall criteria for receiving unemployment payments, however, were tightened. For example, refusing what is deemed acceptable employment, job training, or community services now leads to reduction or even loss of benefits (Ochel 2005). The macroeconomic impact of the reforms on the German labor market are contested among economists. While some argue that the reforms have reduced unemployment significantly, others maintain that their effect on economic recovery has been modest (Hochmuth et al. 2019; Odendahl 2017).

Most importantly for our current analysis, the German government did not move to a workfare model. In fact, on January 1, 2023 a significant reform of the social safety net expanded payments and eased some of the punitive measurements Hartz IV introduced. In an effort to destigmatize welfare payments, the government now refers to *Bürgergeld* (money for citizens) instead of *Sozialgeld*. Rather than "pushing" people into work, the new law emphasizes job training to ensure long-term employment. The welfare system now also covers apartment costs (rent or mortgage) irrespective of its square footage for one year. The community clearly continues to assume responsibility for those who cannot take care of themselves. The worst-case scenario in the Germany system—being a recipient of *Bürgergeld*—still ensures a minimum level of subsistence.[21]

Many scholars have argued that it is it almost impossible to offer truly rehabilitative services from within a punitive framework (Zimring 2005; Fader 2013; Soyer 2016, 2018; Cox 2018). Using a welfare state like Germany as a counterexample to the United States refines this perspective. In southern Germany, the juvenile justice system models rehabilitative measures in prison after social services offered on the outside. For the German group prison is a restrictive experience but it resembles the group's prior encounters with the welfare state (see chapter 2).

The exact opposite is the case in the criminal and juvenile justice system in the United States. To manage those who struggle with the "side effects" of poverty (mental health problems, addiction, lack of education, fractured employment history), the criminal justice system has to create a unique social service infrastructure. Juvenile justice or criminal justice facilities offer educational and mental health support that are out of reach in the community (Soyer 2016; Sufrin 2017; Cox 2018). In a homogenous society like Germany, where "the other" is still assumed to be similar enough to the majority to warrant communal concern, punishment is exercised in form of restrictive social services. Consequently, Germany prisons operate as extensions of the welfare state, while the United States has limited the centralized administration of social welfare to prisons. Spending money on the carceral state is politically far less controversial than allocating expenditures to welfare for the poor. When money is allocated to services in prisons, it is done so under the guise of public safety. Offering social services in prison is also an opportunity to reach a population that would be otherwise cut off from any government support. Finally, the managerial benefits of providing social services in prison cannot be overstated. Group therapy, work, and educational opportunities keep the incarcerated occupied and are a useful disciplinary tool to control a potentially volatile population (Foucault 1975).

While it goes too far to claim that multiculturalism undermines the politics of redistribution (Barry 2001; see Banting and Kymlicka 2004 for a counterargument), universal redistribution of wealth is undoubtedly more difficult to negotiate with opposing interests in play. In terms of population diversity, the United States is a much more complex society than Germany. According to the latest census, almost 14 percent of the US population is foreign-born and only 60 percent of the population define themselves as white non-Hispanic.[22] Out of a population of eighty-three million, only 11.4 million people live in Germany without holding a German passport. Of these, about 4.8 million come from other EU countries while roughly 1.4 million hold Turkish citizenship. From the perspective of the US census measurements of race and ethnicity, the German population largely consists of different shades of white Europeans.[23]

While they are compelling, the historical pathways and cultural idiosyncrasies of punishment and welfare should not be reduced to population homogeneity as the single explanatory variable. Monica Prasad (2012), for example, convincingly argues that the geographic idiosyncrasies of the United States, the vastness of the land, and the fertility of its soil generated a specific brand of social policies designed to manage over-production and collapsing prices rather than resource scarcity. In Germany, the establishment of a welfare state can be interpreted as the result of Otto von Bismarck's reactionary attempt to combat the kind of socialist ideas he believed threatened Prussia's constitutional monarchy (Steinberg 2011). Consequently, juxtaposing Germany's homogeneity with the heterogenous society of the United States does not offer a causal explanation. Instead, the comparative approach provides a new perspective on divergent punitive trajectories. Focusing on population diversity also offers a corrective view on popular narratives that present prisons in Finland, Norway, or Germany as a model for criminal justice reform in the United States.[24] Acknowledging the complexity, size, and diversity of the United States should therefore induce us to speak in a cautionary manner when using European countries as a benchmark for evaluating the American criminal justice.

CONCLUSION

By investigating the tensions between Durkheim's theory and the complex cultural and historical contingencies at play in Germany and the United States, this chapter relativizes the image of Germany as a blueprint for criminal justice reform in the United States. Germany's benevolent criminal justice system was created on the heels of one of the most destructive and brutal political dictatorships ever to have existed. Under the supervision of the Allied forces, Germany reinvented itself as guardian of human rights. Immediately after World War II, German society was more homogenous than ever. Punishment, as well as welfare benefits, were created solely for a community of ethnic Germans. In their collective guilt and trauma Germans relied on a "solidarity of likeness" to rebuild their country. As Germany has become more diversified, however, immigrants and their children have inadvertently benefited from a justice and welfare system built on the assumption of cultural homogeneity. Offering immigrants access to social citizenship and a relatively lenient justice system does not imply that immigration is seen as an asset. On the contrary, immigrants and their children are supposed to assimilate completely while never being considered truly German.[25]

On the surface, the United States could be an almost ideal-typical representation of a society bound by "organic solidarity." And yet successful economic cooperation of people from different ethnic and racial background has not resulted in a more tolerant justice system. The focus on economic success, in the absence of true intersubjectivity, may have, in fact, enabled harsh punitive structures. Not being bound by communal responsibility derived from shared cultural heritage or trauma can make it easier to cast judgment on those who have committed crimes. In the absence of a centralized welfare state, the US criminal justice system has grown enormously. It now executes the kind of social services and disciplining functions Germany has front-loaded to the welfare state.

The tension between Durkheim's theory and the complex reality of punishment in Germany and the United States reveals that the German model does not provide an easy solution for criminal justice reform in the United States. Immigrants in Germany are stigmatized and often thwarted on their path to upward mobility. Residents who have a migration background are expected to assimilate completely to German culture without any expectation that their children or grandchildren ever be considered part of the community. Those advocating for criminal justice reform in the United States therefore need to be aware that less punitive systems do not always presuppose tolerance. Germany and other Nordic countries may have maintained a lenient punishment regime and generous welfare benefits because they remain comparatively small, homogenous societies that mostly take care of those who are like "them" (Lappi-Seppälä 2007). In the following chapters I will explore how these different cultural assumptions, economic realities, and punitive practices shape the respondents' in both countries identity and positionality.

CHAPTER TWO

The Uncertainty of Belonging

Narratives of Difference and Exclusion
in Germany and the United States

American sociologists have presented a variety of hypotheses about the relationship between structure, culture, and social action (Lamont, Beljean, and Clair 2014; Small 2004; Swidler 1986). At the same time, US-based researchers have rarely looked beyond American society to understand the meaning-making processes of disadvantaged populations.[1] In my first book, *A Dream Denied* (2016), for example, I observed that teenagers in Chicago and Boston developed an exaggerated sense of agency while they were held in juvenile detention centers. I interpreted their narratives as a reflection of the myth of the "American Dream" that emphasizes equal access to opportunities. Lacking a counterfactual, however, my argument couldn't definitively connect the teenagers' utterances to the culturally specific environment they grew up in. William Julius Wilson's (1990) hypothesis about cultural values prevailing in inner-city communities is exposed to a similar criticism. Without comparative examples of poor populations living in different social settings, we have to take at face value that cultural isolation and systematic structural disadvantage perpetuate self-sabotaging cultural frames.

This chapter expands the debate about the relationship between culture, inequality, and identity beyond the United States. Setting narratives of incarcerated young men in the United States in relation to a similar group of respondents in Germany allows for a more comprehensive understanding of culture as "webs of significance" (Geertz 2017) that shape the young men's identity and understanding of their role in society.

Given the cultural contingencies of both societies, it is fair to say that the young men in Germany and the United States experience their outsider status very differently. American and German respondents, however, align in describing their marginalization as an individual rather than a social problem (Crewe 2009). The young men's interpretation of their environment testifies to subtle but significant forms of discrimination and marginalization prevalent in both countries. Rather than recollecting dramatic incidents of racism, they relate a more elusive but constant experience of marginalization. In aggregate these microprocesses significantly influence the respondents' self- understanding. Lamont and others have termed these cultural processes of stratification "symbolic inequality." These scripts operate open-endedly and are constructed intersubjectively. They manifest subconsciously but nonetheless entrench the material and ecological aspects of stratification (Lamont, Beljean, and Clair 2014, 581). As result, the young men do not perceive themselves as being discriminated against or treated unfairly. They interpret their social position as an unfortunate combination of self-defeating choices and tragic events beyond their control.

In order to analyze the data I collected comparatively, I needed to contextualize the young men's identity constructions in the historical and cultural environment they grew up in. The construction of the self, as George Herbert Mead (1967) argued, develops in relation to society—the generalized other—and the benchmark for exclusion from or inclusion in the mainstream is very different in Germany than it is in the United States. Before I delve into the young men's narratives, I will briefly summarize the cultural assumptions and structural realities that impact the young men's perception of difference, exclusion, and belonging in both countries.

AN AMERICAN DILEMMA

Acts of police violence against African Americans are only the latest iteration of what Gunnar Myrdal (1995) referred to as the "American Dilemma." Published in 1944, Myrdal's work of the same name described the United States as torn between the rhetoric of opportunity and the brutal reality of Jim Crow laws in the South. As an outsider (Myrdal was from Sweden), Myrdal saw clearly what white Americans were reluctant to admit: Even after the practice of slavery had ended, a majority of African Americans continued to exist in a state of indentured servitude on former plantations in the South. The "Freedman Bureau" failed to make good on the promise of "forty acres and a mule"; and, as W. E. B. Du Bois aptly observed, an African American who became a landowner and achieved upward mobility did so "by the grace of his thrift rather than the bounty of the government" (1994, 20).

Fleeing Southern Jim Crow laws and economic devastation after World War II, the "great migration" of African Americans led to a massive increase of the Black population in Northern industrial cities such as Detroit, Chicago, and Philadelphia. As has been extensively documented elsewhere, moving north did not bring prosperity but led to the creation of segregated and resource deprived inner-city communities (Satter 2009; Conley 2009; Venkatesh 2002; Massey and Denton 1994). Today, segregation remains a social problem that also affects middle-class African American families. In *Black Picket Fences*, Mary Pattillo showed that Black middle-class families are likely to live adjacent to poor neighborhoods. Their children inadvertently share resources with poor families. They attend failing schools and are exposed to crime and violence. Middle-class white children, on the other hand, live far removed from these social ills of poverty (1999).

Recent data confirm that past discriminatory practices continue to impact the net worth of African American families. In 2016, the average African American family had a median net worth of $17,150 compared to a median net worth of $171,150 for white families. Among other factors, white families disproportionately profit from inheritance tax law. Income is taxed at seven times the rate than inherited wealth (Batchelder 2007). The low taxes on inheritances have therefore contributed to sustaining the African American–white wealth gap across generations (Hamilton and Darity 2010).

Mass incarceration has dealt another blow to already embattled minority communities (Alexander 2010). By the mid-2000s African American men under the age of forty were incarcerated at a rate of 11.5 percent. In fact, incarceration had become so common among poorly educated African American men, that the likelihood of experiencing incarceration was twice as high as their probability of receiving government support or joining the army (Western 2006). Most recent data show a narrowing gap of between black and white incarceration rates, while class inequality has increased (Muller and Roehrkasse 2022). Between 2008 and 2018, Black incarceration rates declined by 28 percent. Over the same time frame incarceration rates dropped 2 percent for whites. Despite these encouraging trends, Black men remain 5.8 percent more likely to be incarcerated than white men (Carson 2020). Overall, mass incarceration has increased the economic pressure on already-struggling African American families and has caused irreparable damage to the social fabric of disadvantaged inner-city communities (Wakefield and Wildeman 2013; Wacquant 2009).

In addition to facing structural disadvantages, African Americans have to navigate a rather complex field of subtly racist interactions and stereotyping in their daily lives. "Stereotype thread"—awareness that others expect certain behaviors based on one's race, ethnicity, or gender, has a measurable impact on aspirations and performance (Steele and Aronson 1995). The negative stereotypes circulating about underachievement of African Americans in the United States, for example, significantly impact their test results. Walton and others found that 17 percent to 19 percent of the white/Black gap on the SAT exams can be accounted for by stereotype threat (2013).

The structural and cultural aspects of discrimination in the United States are empirically well-established (Pager 2003). Individual experience with racism and the extent to which race is relevant for one's identity, on the other hand, differs significantly between people. For instance, highly educated African Americans are less likely to have contact with the criminal justice system than those who have not finished high school (Western 2006). At the same time, middle-class African Americans are more likely to occupy the "sole person" role in a predominantly white social setting and therefore experience their race very differently than a teenager living in a segregated inner-city neighborhood (Bobo 2012; Coates 2015).

Finally, like any ethnic group in the United States, African Americans are a heterogeneous crowd. For a number of African Americans their race and culture may not play a prominent role in their identity constructions at all. Others connect to their African American cultural heritage in moderate ways, and some may experience their race and, by extension, being discriminated against as an important aspect of their lives (Cross 1991; Strauss and Cross 2005). As this chapter delves further into the analysis of the interview data, it is important to keep the range of possible identity constructions in mind. The data focus on the identity development of an extremely disadvantaged subset of young men, and the results should not be treated as representative for a population as diverse as African Americans are in the United States.

"It's a fucked-up predicament"

Jeremiah's family was more firmly situated in the middle class than other families I interviewed in Pennsylvania. His grandmother owned a beautiful house on a tree-lined street in West Philadelphia. She had been a foster-mother for two decades when I met her. Money was never there in abundance but she had always found ways to offer her children and grand-children the semblance of a middle-class life. She was especially proud of her daughter—Jeremiah's aunt—who had graduated from an elite college and lived with her husband and two children in a wealthy suburb close to Chicago. Jeremiah's mother was in many ways the exact opposite of her successful sister. She became hooked on drugs and Jeremiah suffered immensely from seeing his mother succumbing to addiction again and again.

In school Jeremiah struggled with ADHD. The Catholic private school he attended was unwilling to accommodate his needs and he ended up attending an underresourced local public school. As a teenager, Jeremiah became involved with a neighborhood gang. During our interviews his enduring fascination with the gang lifestyle was obvious. He recounted a detailed history of the Crips and Bloods and pointed out the different ways his tattoos paid tribute to his involvement in an East Coast offshoot of the Bloods. His grandmother believed that his demeanor was at odds with that of the quiet child she had raised. She also assumed that he embellished his involvement in the gang.

Even though Jeremiah had the unwavering support of his family, he fell behind in school because of his learning disability. He began acting out to compensate for his deficiencies and was labeled a troublemaker. As he grew older, his involvement with the streets continued to escalate and he embraced being a gang member (Soyer 2018). When I spoke to him at SCI Pine Grove, he blamed himself for ending up in prison. Not only did he believe that it was his fault; he had also convinced himself that discrimination had played no role in his trajectory. He made clear that he did not want to "blame it on white people" that he was incarcerated. From his perspective "Black on Black" crime was the problem that haunted inner-city neighborhoods.

He insisted on the irrelevance of racism, even though he had experienced first-hand that his family expanded an extraordinary effort to hold onto their middle-class status. When he spent a summer in the wealthy suburb where his aunt and her family lived, he noticed that his relatives were the only Black family around. He felt "out of place." Being the only Black child at the pool, he was not comfortable jumping in: "My skin get darker while I'm in the sun like right now, and it was just like no."

After being exposed to white upper-middle-class culture he had never experienced before, Jeremiah was not able to code switch effectively (Anderson 1999). It was also difficult for him to perceive the racial disparity as the result of institutionalized discrimination and systematic disadvantage. After all, his aunt and uncle had made it and were accepted members of this white suburban community. After a brief stay in Illinois, he went back to Philadelphia. He felt at home there and being in a gang allowed him to bracket his identity in meaningful ways.

Blake, who was sentenced to one to five years in prison for selling drugs, also tried to make sense of the discrepancy in wealth he noticed in his hometown Harrisburg. He argued that "white people . . . take advantage of going to school." He also insisted that successful white people are not necessarily born into wealth: "I'm pretty sure there's a lot of white people that's out there that [are] CEOs now, that came from nothing. Just like there's a lot of black people out there right now that came from nothing." Trying to ensure that Blake did not simply provide answers he deemed socially desirable, I pointed out the intergenerational wealth white Americans had been able to transmit over centuries. He responded bluntly: "All white people don't got stuff to fall back on. . . . like the trailer park. That's, that's the white version of the hood. That's still the ghetto at the end of the day. That's low income. For real." In the end, Blake believed that white people simply made more realistic plans for their future. As he put it: "See me, black people and Spanish people, . . . they would go to college, say that don't work, their back-up plan be like, oh I wanna get my barber license. . . . That's not the next best thing, that's everybody, everybody in the hood all over America cutting hair. So, why would you [choose that]?"

While Blake knew that his community was in a "fucked-up predicament," he did not want to make excuses for himself. At the beginning of his time in prison he recalled blaming not having a father in his life, or needing money for his actions. Now he believed that he should have found other ways to make ends meet: "You don't always gotta resort to shooting somebody with a gun. You don't gotta always resort to selling drugs. You get a job. You go fight with your hands."

For Jeremiah and Blake taking responsibility for their actions translated into negating structural racism, though they still intuitively understood their disadvantage. The good neighborhoods, they remarked casually—that's where the white people live. Blake knew that white people never found their way to the part of Harrisburg he grew up in, unless they were police or wanted to buy drugs. Jeremiah also noticed that his sister was one of the very few Black girls at her private school located in the suburbs of Philadelphia. He knew that her classmates did not have to struggle like she did:

"My sister have to earn everything that she has, every single thing. . . . Their [the white classmates'] parents pay for that, here you go. Give you $100. Go to school, get lunch money. My sister has to work at a daycare at a young age, manage homework, and getting money for her phone bill."

Mother of Exiles

A self-described country of immigrants, the United States not only has to reckon with their legacy of slavery, but also with its history of discrimination against newcomers. While anyone who is born on American soil is considered a citizen, immigrants and their descendants are not created equal. After initial discrimination against the Irish, Jews, or Italians, the third and fourth generation of European immigrants now reside in integrated neighborhoods. For the most part they also do not present as a distinctive ethnic group anymore (Alba, Logan and Crowder 1997; Bonnett 1998; Alba, Lutz and Vesselinov 2001).

Immigrants from Latin America have not been afforded the same route to assimilation. A recent study by the Pew Research Center (2018) shows that only 45 percent of Americans know that most immigrants reside in the United States legally. A significant number of respondents (also 45 percent) were still under the impression that there is a connection between immigrants and criminal behavior. Even though citizenship does not predict involvement in criminal behavior, men who identify as Latino are overrepresented in the state prison system in comparison to white men. Recent work on sentencing emphasizes that immigrant status may be an even more salient factor than race when it comes to the severity of punishment. Light, Massoglia, and King (2014) show that citizenship has a stronger impact on sentencing than race and ethnicity in federal court. Controlling for citizenship also obliterates the difference in sentencing between Hispanics and whites.

Being a citizen, however, does not protect Latinos from experiencing exclusion. Based on ninety-eight in-depth interviews with Puerto Ricans, Ariana Valle (2019) argues that the legal status of Puerto Ricans in the United States is questioned regularly. They are lumped together with other immigrants from Latin America, especially immigrants from Mexico. Being seen as a "illegitimate," despite their citizenship status, emphasizes the powerful narrative of Latino immigration as qualitatively different from earlier waves of immigrants entering the United States from Europe.

Like African Americans, Latinos continue to live in segregated neighborhoods that afford very little opportunities for advancement (Bourgois 2002; Contreras 2013). Latino men are stigmatized and labeled intensely. Victor Rios describes a "Youth Control Complex" that encompasses the lives of the Latino youths he observed—regardless of their actual involvement in crime (2011). Like African American incarceration rates, Latino incarceration rates have declined. Between 2008 and 2018 the number of Latino inmates in state prison decreased by 21 percent. Nevertheless, the fact that Latinos constitute 23 percent of the state prison population means that they are still overrepresented in the criminal justice system (Carson 2020).[2]

We should again keep in mind that Latinos are a heterogeneous group. When it comes to upward mobility, trajectories differ widely depending on the immigrants' country of origin. Second-generation Central or South Americans, as well as Peruvians, Cubans, and Colombians, even surpass their white peers when it comes to occupational success. The great majority of Latino immigrants, however, stem from Mexico. The lives of the children of Mexican immigrants are still shaped by the stigma of "illegality" and segregation (Gonzales 2015). First-generation Mexican immigrants' legal status, the comparatively low level of their education, and a negative reception environment in the United States contribute to the comparative lack of upward mobility of their children and grandchildren (Van Tran 2016).

Similar to the African American respondents, the Latino young men I interviewed are not a representative sample of the Latino population in the United States. Instead, their narratives offer a specific perspective on the identity development of young Latino men who grew up in segregated inner-city communities.

"Americans can do no wrong"

When I interviewed Jesus in prison, he was twenty years old. He had been raised by his grandmother, who came from Puerto Rico to the continental United States when she was a child. The family first settled in New Jersey but then quickly moved to Philadelphia, where all his grandmother's children and grandchildren were born. Jesus is keenly aware of how his life has been defined by poverty and segregation. For him, being in a prison is not a lot different from living in his neighborhood: "You're really confined in the hood to your own environment. . . . Me being in prison in my cell is no different than being out there because I felt like I was confined out there," he explained.

As the only US respondent who had been enrolled in a four-year college, he observed that underresourced neighborhoods can sap aspirations. Instead of becoming doctors or lawyers, "people just get fucked by their environment." Even though he knew that poverty warped the life courses of those around him, he rejected describing himself as a victim of these circumstances: "I can't blame it [his life course] on the environment. We [people in his neighborhood] fucked each other over. Instead of bringing each other up, we was just encouraging and motivating each other to continue doing the same old bullshit." When he was a child, Jesus was captivated by the self-destruction of heroin addicts around him and he began stashing heroin for his cousins. For him, the essence of drug dealing is "You making money and watching somebody fuck up their life."

Even though Jesus enjoyed going to elementary school, his grandmother encouraged him to act like he had ADHD. She told him to misbehave so that he could become eligible for social security payments. According to Jesus it worked out and his grandmother was able to use his SSI checks to supplement the household income until he was sent to juvenile placement in his mid-teens. Jesus was convinced that many other families in his neighborhood received social security payments illegitimately as well: "You just see it with a lot of minorities for real. Cause you don't see that with um, with a white family. I don't know, [with] minorities you see that shit all the time."

While he believed his grandmother's choices were wrong, he acknowledged the limited agency she had vis-à-vis the government agencies that intervened in his life. Jesus recalled that she never questioned the different therapeutic interventions that he was exposed to. In his grandmother's eyes, "Americans can do no wrong . . . if they would have told her like yeah, like make him jump off a bridge, she probably would have went along with it because somebody else told her it was good for me."

During our final interview, it became evident that his narrative of individual responsibility was connected to his fear of not being able to live an independent life away from the streets. Emphasizing that he and others in in his neighborhood were responsible for their actions implied that he had control over his fate. Jesus knew it would be difficult for him to find a job quickly after his release. He speculated that failing to secure employment might draw him back to the streets, and he was uncertain what the future might hold for him. Jesus explained that he had always wanted to run his own business. But now he was not so sure anymore. Half-jokingly, he added at the end of our interview, "I'm having a mid-life crisis."

While Jesus was born on the mainland, Mateo's family moved from Puerto Rico to Allentown, Pennsylvania when he was twelve years old. "My mom—she was trying to get a better life," he explained. From his perspective moving to Allentown had been a net benefit for his family. He considered Puerto Rico his home, but remembered the neighborhood he lived in as a violent and drug-infested place. Mateo believed that people in Puerto Rico "don't got a lot of benefits and hope . . ." Mateo did not speak English when he arrived but, by his own account, he picked the language up quickly. He also recalled that his family was poor even though both his parents worked. While he understood his family's disadvantage, he mostly blamed himself for ending up in prison: "I started hanging out with wrong people, start[ed] getting locked up, fighting in school, getting kicked out of school." Like his uncle, who was a member of the Latin Kings, Mateo became a gang member. He joined "for the loyalty. For the love they show you. . . . They help you with anything you need. Help your family."

When Mateo reflected on why he ended up being sentenced to two to five years for aggravated assault, he did not feel resentment toward the system that had adjudicated him. Instead, he talked about feeling angry with his father who started out as a "big drug dealer in Puerto Rico," but ended up getting hooked on dope himself. From Mateo's perspective his father never raised him or gave him anything. He and his mother had violent fights. Mateo remembered that everyone in his family always argued about money. When his father found out that Mateo had been sent to prison, he returned to Puerto Rico. Mateo sent him a letter from prison but never received a reply. In the end, Mateo believed his father did not want to confront his son's incarceration.

In his recollections Mateo's challenging family dynamic overshadowed any other structural difficulties he might have encountered as he tried to integrate into life in his new hometown. His families' ties to the Latin Kings also made it easy for him to turn to the gang for recognition and support. His gang involvement not only compensated for difficulties at home but also allowed him to feel connected to a place whose language and customs he was not familiar with.

Mateo and Jesus focused on their individual challenges over lager socioeconomic mechanisms disadvantaging Latino families in the United States. They mostly remembered their families' struggles from a microlevel perspective, and framed their current situation as a result of their own actions, or the failings of adults in their life.

Personal Responsibility and Structural Disadvantage

It is tempting to frame the narratives of the US respondents' as a sign of alienation and false consciousness (Gaventa 1982). This simplified Marxian interpretation, however, *does not* do justice to the complex reality the respondents had to navigate. Jeremiah and Blake understood that their neighborhoods were deprived of resources. Jesus also realized that his Puerto Rican grandmother was not able to read "American" society correctly. She couldn't advocate as effectively for him as a white middle-class mother or grandmother would have been able to. Likewise, Mateo observed that his parents worked hard but still struggled financially.

Jesus's, Mateo's, Blake's, and Jeremiah's denial of systemic racism simply allowed them to uphold their illusion of agency.

Imagining themselves as uninhibited by discrimination also enabled them to retain a modicum of dignity and optimism.

Their perspective on American society was also impacted by their individual traumatic experiences (Soyer 2018). As children they had witnessed repeatedly that adults' drug use and violence made their family's situation worse. Jeremiah, for example, could not possibly understand his mother's drug use in terms of his country's history of slavery and racism. From a child's perspective, she simply let him down, while his aunt and grandmother were proof that she could have chosen differently. The individual, visceral experience of trauma and disappointment therefore obfuscated the undercurrent of systemic racism that undeniably impacted their communities.

THE GERMAN QUESTION

In Germany, the history of racism predates the founding of the United State by centuries.[3] Historically, Germans have defined belonging to the Volk (the people) by ancestry and culture rather than territory (Anderson 1991). The predecessor of the German Reich, the Holy Roman Empire, consisted of a multitude of quasi-sovereign chiefdoms, lordships, and kingdoms. Germany—a "delayed nation" (Plessner 2001)—became a coherent territory long after France, Great Britain, or the United States.[4] To compensate for the absence of a nation state, Germans, Hannah Arendt (1944) argued, developed a specific "race-thinking." Instead of territorial unity, they emphasized their racial unity.

When Bismarck succeeded in creating a unified Germany under the hegemony of Prussia, he did so with the significant support of his Jewish banker Gerson Bleichroeder (Stern 1977).

At the same time, however, the Jewish population was never considered an integral part of Germany. Jews remained "strangers," even though Germans and Jews had shared the same territory for centuries and Jewish artists and philosophers had embodied German culture (Stern 1977; Elon 2002; Simmel 1971).[5] Historians and social scientists agree that Nazi ideology did not emerge suddenly in 1933, and that it did not suddenly end with the surrender of the German army on May 8, 1945. Hitler's antisemitism in many ways seamlessly connected to a specific kind of exclusive messianic nationalism that had been simmering at least since the nineteenth century and was embraced by the highest echelons of German society during the Weimar Republic (Karlauf 2020; Adorno 2019; Korn 1999; Kracauer 1984).

During the 1940s, when Gunnar Myrdal was traveling through the United States recording the hypocrisy of American society, the Nazi leadership relentlessly pursued its goal of the complete destruction of European Jewry (Hilberg 1999). During the height of the killings in Eastern Europe, between July 1942 and November 1942, more than one million people died in the gas chambers of Belzec, Sobibor, and Treblinka alone (Stone 2019). The Holocaust was a crime of such massive proportions that the German language developed a specific term capturing the process of coming to terms with the collective guilt of the German people: *Vergangenheitsbewältigung*.

Under the leadership of the first postwar chancellor, Konrad Adenauer, German society defined itself mostly through its efforts to rebuild the country and the desire to enter the international political stage once again. Germany at once distanced itself from the Third Reich, while relentlessly reintegrating former Nazis at the familial, social, and political levels of society (Perels 2004; Welzer 2002; Mommsen 1991).[6] As part of the German efforts to present the country as a peaceful and trustworthy nation, race as a category was erased from the German vocabulary. Instead of racial unity, Germans emphasized a set of cultural norms and values that defined their society. Replacing race with the notion of culture (including democracy and liberalism) was supposed to imply tolerance. However, insisting on assimilation to German culture has continued to ostracize those who seem not share this particular Western European, Christian perspective (Yurdakul and Korteweg 2013; Korteweg 2014; Oers 2021).

The first immigrants who entered postwar Germany were the so-called *Gastarbeiter*, who came to the newly established Federal Republic to address the shortage of laborers during the postwar economic boom. Recruited from Southern European countries and Turkey, these workers were not supposed to settle in Germany. Chartered trains delivered these men, who were treated as a commodity, directly from their home country to the German companies desperate for a cheap labor force. Their initial living quarters were provisional barracks provided by the companies that had recruited them. In 1973, when labor recruitment officially ended, those who were supposed to be temporary "guests" had turned into permanent immigrants. Despite these "guests'" having experienced an unfriendly reception environment, their families had followed them, and Germany had to come to terms with a significant immigrant population. Over time, the status of "foreigners" who had settled permanently in Germany was tackled legislatively. The political establishment abandoned the idea of forcibly resettling workers to their country of origin. After all, the German constitution granted civil and individual rights to everyone irrespective of nationality (Joppke 1999, 63–85).

It took much longer to dispose of the traditional notion that the German nation was bound by blood and not territory. Until January 1, 2000, when a reformed citizenship law went into effect, the children of those workers who were born and raised in Germany did not have a clear path to German citizenship. Access to German citizenship was defined by the principles of ius sanguinis (Brubaker 1992). Having German ancestors guaranteed citizenship irrespective of where a person resided. Although immigrants from Turkey, Italy, Greece, and Yugoslavia fulfilled an important economic function, their grandchildren born on German soil were still considered foreigners (*Ausländer*) (Partridge 2012). Children born in Germany to immigrant parents prior to the reform of the citizenship law received the citizenship of their parent's country of origin.

Even though the new citizenship law moved in the direction of ius soli, the outsider status of many German respondents continued to be defined by the old concept of ius sanguinis. A majority of the young men I interviewed were born just before the legal changes took effect. Their extensive criminal history prevented other paths to naturalization and minimized their chances of becoming citizens in the future. Those who had a long history of criminal behavior were at risk of being deported to the country their parents or even grandparents came from decades ago (Narimani 2017).

In contrast to the United States, the German census does not record ethnicity. Instead, the census bureau collects information on the diffuse category of "migration background." This rubric also includes German citizens born in Germany whose families immigrated to Germany generations ago. About 21.3 million people fall into this category.[7] Given the homogeneity of German society, it is not a surprise that the citizenship reform did not change the narrow definition of what it means to truly belong to German society. In the early 2000s, a female teacher in Baden-Württemberg insisted on wearing the headscarf in public school, which put her at odds with the school administrators and the ministry of education. The now infamous "headscarf debate" revealed that wearing a headscarf as a sign of being Muslim was still irreconcilable with being German (Korteweg and Yurdakul 2013).

"But I am German"

Arslan spent a total of six years in various locked facilities in Baden-Württemberg. His latest charge was for an attempted second-degree murder. He fractured the skull of another person incarcerated at JVA Adelsheim because he had called Arslan a "son of a whore."

Arslan's mother immigrated from Turkey with her parents when she was thirteen years old. His father was born in Germany as a son of guest workers who came in the 1960s. Arslan was twelve years old when his father died of lung cancer. Since his family had lived in Germany for two generations, he felt removed from his Turkish heritage: "When I have children there will not be a lot of Turk left in them," he joked.

During our first interview in prison, I revealed my own biases and asked him: How was it to grow up Turkish in Stuttgart? Arslan was not faced by assumptions about his identity and he simply replied: "But I am German." He added that people always thought he had a "migration background" because of his dark hair and darker skin. Apparently, I was not the only one who presumed that someone who looked like him could not possibly be a German citizen. Arslan also explained that people often believed he was joking when he referred to himself as German. On the other hand, identifying as Turkish did not feel right to him either: "I have received everything from Germany. I was born in Germany. I can't just say: I am Turkish." Arslan therefore preferred to consider himself German-Turkish.

In the summer of 2019, when I conducted our final interview, Arslan was looking forward to a vacation in Izmir. He loved spending time there and jokingly posed the question: "Why would I live in Germany when I can go to Izmir?" Despite his enthusiasm about vacationing in Turkey, he remained uncertain about whether or not he could live there permanently. For him feeling at home was primarily connected to his mother. This also meant that if his family were to move to Turkey, he would likely leave as well: "I don't have anything left here," he said, adding, "They really fucked me with that five-year sentence." Eventually Arslan settled on a compromise: He loved Germany as a country but hated everything connected to the German state that had locked him up.

Interactions with the police in particular had affirmed that his presence in Germany was considered problematic. Arslan recalled that a police officer claimed he had resisted arrest. From Arslan's perspective the officer simply struggled with putting handcuffs on him. Although he insisted that he did not try to obstruct the officer, Arslan was convinced that nobody believed his version of the event: Come on," he told me, "someone who looks like me and who has been in prison—[. . .] why would anybody believe me?"

Arslan's hybrid identity epitomized the situation of young people born to immigrant families after the citizenship law reform. Children born in Germany after January 2000 are eligible for German citizenship similar to a child born on US soil.

Arslan not only held a German passport; he did not even have Turkish citizenship. His actual citizenship status, however, was irrelevant when it came to other people's perspective on his status as a "foreigner." His experience of exclusion had left him deeply ambivalent about the country of his birth. Especially after he experienced how correctional officers spoke to him and others in prions, he concluded the following: "In every German is a little bit of a . . ." While he did not finish his sentence, we both knew the term that was left unspoken was *Nazi*.[8]

Carlo, whose father was of African descent, experienced being racially profiled on a regular basis in his hometown. Carlo grew up in Freiburg—a small university town in the Black Forest. Like Arslan, he was a German citizen. In his experience, the police never stopped those who looked ethnically German but always targeted him and his friends who had darker skin and appeared to have a "migration background." Carlo had been sentenced to three years for aggravated assault. He was ashamed of what he had done and did not want to talk about how he had ended up in prison. I asked him if the police had ever said anything discriminatory—for example, whether they had used racial slurs. He replied that he had never experienced that, but it was obvious to him that the police considered those who had darker skin to be more dangerous. He also believed that his older white half brothers were profiled because they socialized with a group of Roma, a population generally considered to be involved in organized crime.[9] While the police never used racial slurs, strangers on the street did not hold back when they encountered him and called him "n . . . . r."[10] He did not want to paint himself as a victim: "When I was younger it really upset me, but now I don't care anymore," he explained.

Just like in Carlo's and Arslan's cases, Marko's dark skin meant that he was immediately identified as not being ethnically

German. Marko's parents are Roma; they came to Germany more than thirty years ago. The family first settled in Hannover, in northern Germany. Marko was born there, but when he was about five years old his parents decided to move to southern Germany. Marko described this relocation as an attempt to get away from family drama that had unfolded in Hannover. His parents were not German citizens, but they held the German equivalent of a Green Card. This allowed them to remain in the country indefinitely without any restrictions. Because of his criminal history Marko had been threatened with deportation to Serbia, the country that had issued his passport. He believed that a six-page letter he wrote to the judge overseeing his immigration case ultimately prevented his deportation. Although he was allowed to remain in Germany for now, Marko expected that he would never be able to receive the kind of unconditional residency permit his parents had.

As a Roma Marko is part of a minority that has faced discrimination all over Europe (McGarry 2014; Ciaian and Kancs 2018; Kende et al. 2021). In Germany the derogatory term *Zigeuner* (gypsy) remains a common moniker. For centuries German literature has styled Zigeuner as a threat to society. They are depicted as criminals, robbers, and kidnappers of children (Solms 2008). Marko insisted, though, that his family has been accepted into the small southern German village they settled in after they left Hannover. The native Germans living in this part of southern Germany are referred to as Swabians and they speak a distinctive local dialect called Swabian. One stereotype about the Swabians is that they are very frugal, bordering on being embarrassingly cheap. Marko referred to this stereotype when he explained that the Swabian neighbors had no hesitation knocking on his family's door when they needed to borrow tools or flour. When someone from his family had to borrow tools in return, the neighbors were happy to reciprocate. Marko's tongue-in-cheek depiction of village dynamics implied that the cheap nature of the Swabians outweighed their racist instinct to treat their Roma neighbors as social pariahs. He even joked that his parents had assimilated to the Swabian way of life completely since they also saved rather than spent their money.

Although Marko affirmed acceptance of his family, he recalled that his former supervisor referred to him as a Zigeuner. He claimed it was mostly in good fun: "I used to call my boss potato." He conceded that some people have said "stupid" stuff. Although he believed that his treatment was not undeserved since that he had not been a particularly "nice guy." Despite the stereotypes about Roma, Marko never concealed his identity: "I have nothing to be ashamed of," he asserted.

Similarly to Arslan and Carlo, Marko also remained uncertain about his acceptance in German society: Other Germans, he believed, would likely not consider him a "model German citizen" (*Vorzeigedeutsche*). After his release, he planned on entering an arranged marriage with a woman who lived in Germany but who, like him, came from a Roma family. Marko related that his family's expectations were more traditional in terms of gender roles. Marrying a German woman unfamiliar with his cultural heritage would have gravely disappointed his parents. Even though Marko was committed to Romani cultural traditions, he also embraced his German identity. He spoke German without a traceable accent and, while he was set to marry within the Roma community, he planned on settling with his future wife in Germany.

Arslan, Marko, and Carlo came from very different ethnic backgrounds. In the eyes of the German majority, their appearance—most importantly their darker skin, marked them as "foreigners." Despite their different citizenship statuses, all three had internalized that they could never be "fully" German—irrespective of how long ago their families had settled in Germany. Although German society identified them as "the other," the young men wanted to stay in Germany. As Arslan remarked, being born and raised in Germany was part of his self-understanding. While he enjoyed going on vacation in Izmir he was aware that he did not belong there either.

In *Unwanted*, Sandra Bucerius (2014) observed that her German-Turkish respondents compensated their exclusion from German society by identifying fiercely with the part of Frankfurt they had grown up in. Almost twenty years later, this new generation of immigrant children and grandchildren did not anchor their identity in a specific locale. In contrast to Bucerius's group, a majority lived in homogenous small-town communities. Their families stood out as "the Turks," "the Blacks," or the "Gypsies." Countering these simplistic categories of "otherness," the young men assumed a "hybrid identity," claiming a liminal space of hyphenated Germanness. By embracing the complexity of their dual identity, these young men inadvertently challenged centuries of hegemonic assumptions about what it means to be part of the German nation (Bhabha 1994; Brubaker 1992).

CONCLUSION

Comparing the narratives of the German and American respondents reflects the different cultural and structural mechanism of exclusion in both countries. The Latino and African American young men I interviewed grew up in a much more diverse society than the German respondents did. The most recent census data of the United States estimates that 13.1 percent of the population identifies as African American and 18.5 percent classify themselves as Hispanic or Latino.[11] Jeremiah and Jesus could be much more confident in their American identity than Arslan and Marko in their "Germanness." The fundamental questions of belonging to American society never emerged during our conversations. As a multiethnic nation, the United States allows the young men to identify with their racial and ethnic identity without "officially" compromising their Americanness. From a legal standpoint, all respondents were American citizens and so were their parents and grandparents. Unsurprisingly, not even Latino respondents expressed the same kind of uncertainty about belonging that was common in the German group.

The ethnic diversity of the United States, as well as the comparatively straightforward access to citizenship, masks the well-known reality of residential segregation. Paradoxically, the African American and Latino respondents had very limited opportunities to interact with white middle- or upper-middle-class peers (Massey 2020; Shedd 2015; Massey and Denton 1994). As a result, their identity construction took place in relation to the minority communities they were part of. The young men focused on the deficits they perceived in their communities. At times they drew conclusions about their own behavior that came astonishingly close to Oscar Lewis's (1975) infamous "culture of poverty" argument. Segregation, mass incarceration, and poverty meant that the discrimination was at once more visceral but less apparent in the day-to-day interactions of the US-based respondents. They were torn between recognizing the extreme structural disadvantage of their communities and interpreting self-defeating choices as cultural dysfunction.

German respondents, in turn, were aware that their "migration background" put them at odds with the majority of ethnic

Germans. They downplayed being discriminated against, even though anti-immigrant political discourse had become more openly hostile during the time in which they came of age. In a comparative analysis of immigrant rights and political processes in European countries Koopemans and others argue that expansion of citizenship rights for immigrants was met with an electoral backlash and the rise of right-wing parties (2013). To the authors, Germany was a notable exception, as the country's past still favored suppression of neofascist rhetoric. Less than a decade later, Germany does not defy these patterns anymore. The right-wing party, AfD (Alternative für Deutschland), has gained significant ground in state, federal, and local elections. The young men assert their self-understanding as German + X (Turkish, Albanian, Polish, etc.) against the backdrop of a persistent cultural narrative that indefinitely precludes their full belonging in German society.

The comparative approach reveals how historical and cultural idiosyncrasies warp the identity of young men at the margins of society. While the American respondents focused on rationalizing away their structural disadvantage, German participants needed to come to terms with their perpetual status as interlopers in an ethnically homogenous society. Both groups did not blame social structures, inherited disadvantaged, or racism. Instead, they focused on maintaining their agency and hope for the future. In Germany, immigrant children construct a hybrid self, while German society hardly registered the nuances of their identity.

The young men in the United States similarly negated the existence of structural racism as they recounted how segregation shaped their upbringing. Respondents in both countries understood that they are systemically disadvantaged and "othered." Being in their late teens or early twenties, these young men simply needed to believe that their past experiences did not define their future. As a way of creating meaning for themselves, they emphasized what they hoped could be possible rather than giving into hopelessness and resignation.

CHAPTER THREE

"Here I get three meals a day"

Segregation and the Relative Experience of Poverty

As was made clear in the preceding chapter, different cultural assumptions about belonging inevitably impacted the respondents' sense of self and their experience of difference. Similarly, American and German respondents also assessed their socioeconomic status in relation to the standard of living they observed in their immediate environment. Growing up in segregated neighborhoods, the young men in the United States lacked comparative examples of peers who lived comfortably in the middle class. German participants, who grew up surrounded by middle-class prosperity, noticed their families' marginalization more clearly. Different benchmarks of need also shaped the young men's pathways into crime, as well as their perspectives on incarceration. In contrast to the childhood narratives of the US respondents, none of the German participants reported housing insecurity or food scarcity. The young men in Germany explained their criminal behavior by pointing to psychological strain caused by familial dysfunctions or unexpected personal tragedies, such as parental death or illness. They did *not* frame committing crimes as way of providing for their families' basic needs.

The German young men, like their American counterparts, aspired to a lifestyle that was out of reach for families of their class position. Yet, even as the American respondents desired mundane aspects of middle-class life, they did not compare their childhood experiences to middle- or upper-middle-class children. An upper-middle-class family making $250,000 can feel "Manhattan poor" in the über-wealthy environment of New York City's Upper East Side.[1] Likewise, living in segregated and disadvantaged neighborhoods, the American young men did not experience their exclusion as drastically as some of the German respondents did (Shedd 2015).

In her groundbreaking book *The Second Shift*, Arlie Hochschild argued that women compare themselves to friends of similar socioeconomic status to evaluate the qualities and deficiencies of their husbands (1989). The young men in this study also measured their living standards in relation to others in their immediate social environment. The German respondents lived among middle-class and upper-middle-class children. The lifestyle of these much wealthier families was the baseline they used to make sense of their own experience (Bucerius 2014). In the United States, middle-class children hardly entered the respondents' immediate life-world. Although they may have passed through wealthier parts of their hometown (Leverentz 2020), in their neighborhood they only encountered people who struggled to get by. In Pennsylvania poverty ran so deep that some children perceived prison as a relief from the suffering they had lived through at home.

DESPERATION AND ASPIRATION:
THE AMERICAN EXPERIENCE

Several respondents in Pennsylvania remembered days when they went hungry because there was not enough food for them to eat at home.[2] Bryan, who had already served two years of his two- to five-year sentence he received for carrying a firearm, remembered the extreme poverty he grew up in: "It'd be hard like when, one week there'd be food on the table for all of us. Then the next day, it'd be a certain amount of food on the table for a number of us. And we ugh, damn. We ate, but not as much as everybody else, you know? We had to take turns on like, on who was gonna get a certain amount this week."

When he was young, Bryan explained, he committed crimes to take care of himself while his mother struggled to feed the family. During his teenage years, his criminal behavior reached a new level. He committed his first armed robbery at fourteen and began selling drugs. At that point, he readily admitted that he was drawn to the lifestyle and the excitement that came from committing crimes. When I asked him if he had any positive memories from his childhood he would like to share, he simply replied: "I wish I had some."

Blake also believed that he was drawn to the streets because he realized how hard his single mother had to work—and how comparatively easy it was to make money selling drugs. The twenty-two-year-old recalled that his family received some welfare payments and food stamps, but this was not enough to cover the bills. His mother had to work two more jobs to make ends meet. Looking back, Blake was unaware of his family's disadvantage. Given the level of poverty he grew up around in Harrisburg, his understanding of what it meant to be poor was calibrated differently: The homeless who lived in squalid conditions were poor. "We wasn't that," he said, "but we was poor. 'Cause we was living, we, we didn't have a house and car and ... all that extra shit. To me, now that I think about it, we was poor. We wasn't middle-class."

While it was especially those respondents who grew up in cities like Pittsburgh, Harrisburg, or Philadelphia who lived close to middle-class or upper-middle-class areas, their life-world never overlapped with their white middle-class peers in significant ways (Pattillo 1999). These young men only understood how poor they had been after the fact, or when coincidences in their lives led to interactions with upper-middle-class families. Gabriel, for example, became aware of how other people lived when his family stayed at a homeless shelter located in a predominantly white, middle-class area. As he recalled:

> The school I went to was a bunch of white people. My middle school was a bunch of white people, there was only a couple black people there. . . . This white dude was my friend, I used to go over to his house all the time, and then that's when I started seeing stuff. Seeing people, like they used to take me out places. . . . They had like a summer house out there [in Myrtle Beach], and they used to take me out there with them. Yeah. That's when I started seeing like there's other stuff out in the world than what I be seeing. I was like eleven years old, twelve, that's what I remember. I used to want them to be my mom and dad 'cause they was cool.

Jaxon, another young Black man from Harrisburg, was used to eating lunch at school but he usually missed out on breakfast because he was late. At home, meal sizes were small: "It wouldn't be a nice sized amount [of food], it'd be a small amount where we couldn't even get full," he explained. Jaxon had cycled through numerous juvenile justice facilities before he was sent to SCI Pine Grove. In fact, he had committed the robbery he was incarcerated for, while he was on the run from his final juvenile placement. Jaxon remembered only one non-punitive social service intervention from his childhood: Through the school district he lived in, he was assigned a woman as his "Therapeutic Staff Support" (TSS). The TSS was supposed to monitor his behavior in school. Although he realized that having someone beside him was nothing to be proud of, he enjoyed spending time with her. He recalled doing "fun stuff" with him like eating out or going to play basketball.

In addition to experiencing food insecurity, several respondents faced housing insecurity. Miguel slept on park benches when his mother did not let him come home. The twenty-one-year-old believed that he had no social or familial support on the outside. Being homeless and having to worry about food and shelter inevitably impacted how he perceived his situation in prison. Compared to sleeping outside or bouncing around between friends and relatives, he appreciated the "comforts" incarceration had to offer. "This is honestly the most stable I've been," he explained, "I don't have to worry about coming home and the doors being locked and I can't get into my house to go to sleep." Having regular access to food was a benefit as well. As Miguel put it: "Here, I get three meals a day which I wasn't promised in the streets. You know? . . . I'm not glad that I'm here but it's helpful for me to be more stable than I was in the streets."

Gabriel did not have to sleep on park benches, but his family passed through several homeless shelters. Living in Pittsburgh, the temporary housing they were assigned in that city was usually located in its most disadvantaged neighborhoods. Facing an unstable living situation made it almost impossible for him to study. Staying at a shelter, he explained, "it's hard to do your schoolwork, because there's so many people living in one place: "It's just difficult to do stuff with people running around."

Gabriel's family remained in temporary housing right until he was finished with fifth grade. He remembered being angry and ashamed that his mother could not afford to live in a regular apartment. When the school bus picked him up, other children would make fun of where he lived.

Like Gabriel, Connor was worried about how other children perceived him. He grew up in Erie and described himself as mixed-race. His case summary file plainly identified him as African American. When I interviewed him, he was twenty years old and two years into his three- to ten-year sentence for robbery. He appeared much younger and his demeanor was that of a child in a man's body. After Connor's parents divorced, they had to move frequently because his mother didn't always pay the rent. Knowing he could not control whether or not his mother had enough money to cover the bills, Connor worried about how others perceived him. He did not want to be made fun of because he was wearing second-hand clothing. It made him feel good to wear the newest items in front of his classmates, and when he couldn't afford to purchase them, he simply stole them from department stores.

The young men in Germany also reported that they used to steal items they couldn't afford, but the US sample more clearly expressed the desire to consume conspicuously (Merton 1938; Messner and Rosenfeld 2007). Tyler, a twenty-two-year-old Black man, who was raised by his grandmother in Harrisburg, used to admire his uncles. As a child he believed that they were successful drug dealers. Like them, Tyler wanted to drive expensive cars and be seen with the beautiful women that seemed to be attracted to those vehicles. "I was like, alright, I want that," he said. Now he just felt "dumb" for falling for this superficial display of wealth. After three years in prison he saw things differently: "In the end," he said, "you gotta pay for it all. At the end, it don't mean nothin.'"

Given the extreme deprivation many of the American respondents lived through, making a lot of money quickly was a compelling prospect for them. Kayden, who moved back and forth between North Carolina and Central Pennsylvania growing up, used to live with his mother and his sister in public housing. For him, the drug dealers were the only people he knew who had money to spend. When he was growing up, he thought: "I wanna be like him one day. Getting money like selling drugs, stuff like that." In his early twenties, with two children of his own and serving a two- to four-year sentence for robbery, he was now worried that people might think of him as "being some hard ass." Kayden explained that he always tried to present himself as someone he is not: "I've got a heart," he said, "I sometimes wear a mask."

Kayden and others framed their behavioral choices as a mix of desperation and aspiration. They desired to live "normal" lives but they were so far removed from any middle-class stability that they could not conceptualize a normative process of upward mobility (Young 2004). Facing hunger, eviction, and neighborhood violence, they identified with the local drug dealers. After spending years in prison, many felt they had reached a dead end. Even though they were only in their early twenties, living a comfortable life was more out of reach for them than ever.

THE "GILDED AGE"

Philadelphia, the largest city in Pennsylvania, exemplifies the divisions between the haves and have-nots that are spatially proximate but that hardly intersect with each other in their daily lives. Philadelphia, one of the oldest cities in the country, is home to several universities and colleges, among them the University of Pennsylvania. Founded in 1740, the University of Pennsylvania (Penn), like Harvard and Princeton, is part of the Ivy League. During the academic year of 2021–22, attending such a storied institution of higher learning came with a price tag of $83,298 for students who resided on campus.[3] The university is a thirty-minute subway ride from one of the most disadvantaged areas of the city—Kensington. Jesus, who grew up in that neighborhood, offered a harrowing description of his childhood in Kensington and his way into drug dealing:

Me and my cousins used to walk to school at the age of seven by ourselves. So, it was like six, seven, eight blocks from my house to the school. And from that, from the time we walked out of the house, all the blocks we passed, literally on every corner would be a drug corner. Whether it was crack, everything on one corner. But all the same drugs would be on the next corner. And you would see kids, like thirteen, hustling out there. Selling chains, watches, and you thinking damn here I am going to school and they out here making money. And the only thing school really, I don't know. I like education, but school don't give you everything that's really gonna help you in life. Things that you learn in school, the reading and math, that's all you really need from school. Everything, all that calculus and other shit, I ain't never gonna use it. Mostly everybody in Philly ain't gonna use it, unless they be like that percentage that's probably gonna make it somewhere. And I be walking to school from like eight years old, nine years old to be like I'm gonna start hustling. So I started hanging around my older cousins after school. Looking at them, seeing how they interact with fiends, the drug addicts. And then one day, I'm like let me get what you got in your pocket. Like hustling, they calling that trapping. I'm like yeah, I wanna trap. So, they gave me the drugs and told me to stash it. So, I stashed it. And a fiend, like my first fiend came up and they wanted a bag of heroin for $10. Like you got dope, what's the stamp on it? I'm like yeah, I got dope from such and such. He wanted the stash, I gave it to him. Ever since that $10 stash, I just, I just loved it. I don't know why. It was just interacting with so many people. 'Cause while I was hustling like even at, even recently and I looked around. I used to interact with the fiends, like why the fuck is he doing this? You see females pregnant, bring their kids up to you. You know the kids is starving and all that. Yet, they still coming to spend their money, like you gotta stamp?

Jesus's depiction of poverty and excessive drug use is not an exaggeration. According to a community brief put together by Drexel University Urban Health Collaborative, the average income per capita was $12,669 per year between 2012 and 2016 (Confair et al. 2019). While some of the students at the University of Pennsylvania receive full scholarships, the majority of students are drawn from the top 10 percent of the income bracket. Based on data collected between 1997 and 2013, the median family income of a University of Pennsylvania student was $195,000 (Chetty et al. 2017).[4]

Reminiscent of the Gilded Age, the University of Pennsylvania's endowment reached $20.5 billion in June 2021.[5] Around the same time, the city of Philadelphia tried to clear Kensington of homeless encampments, which, according to activists, may hold about six hundred people during the summer. Even as Kensington's streets were cleared of the mentally ill and drug addicts, the city government conceded that they could offer very little as an alternative. Local residents were resigned and simply expected new encampments to crop up again shortly after the old ones had been demolished.[6]

COMFORTABLE EXCLUSION: THE GERMAN EXPERIENCE

By all measures, the German respondents grew up in a more secure and more comfortable environment. Like the American sample, the German group judged their own social status in relation to their environment. In accordance with Sandra Bucerius's analysis in her 2014 book *Unwanted*, this new generation of teenagers felt poor in comparison to children who lived in households where both parents were ethnically German. The young men in Germany did not experience abject poverty but, in comparison to the majority of German society, their families were disadvantaged and excluded. My interview took place about sixteen years after Bucerius conducted her study. Given the political and structural change German society underwent between the early 2000s and 2016, it is remarkable that the young men felt excluded in the same way their parents' generation did (Bucerius 2014, 15).

Armend was born in Germany after his parents fled Kosovo during the war in the late 1990s. His father's addiction to slot machines led the family into poverty and further displacement. Even though his father was working every day, the family couldn't pay rent. Armend even remembered that his father seized his sister's salary she had earned working as a nurse aid in a psychiatric hospital. When she refused to hand the money over to him, he became violent. In comparison to other German respondents, Armend's family lived under very difficult circumstances. Dependent on government housing, they stayed in a trailer and had to share a kitchen and bathroom with several single men, who struggled with drug and alcohol addiction as well. Despite their challenging living situation, though, they never had to worry about food and shelter.

Growing up without the fear of homelessness and hunger may explain why German respondents did not frame their criminal behavior in terms of the need to provide for their families' basics needs. Armend, for example, believed that the crimes he had committed were driven by his struggles with addiction. He plainly stated that he committed theft because he needed the money to buy drugs and alcohol. According to his case file,

Armend was sentenced for grand larceny, damage to property, and harassment. He remained in Adelsheim for about a year and six months. The social workers in prison were aware of his difficult homelife, and Armend was offered a place in a nonpunitive group home after he was released. He refused to go there because he did not want to be away from his mother any longer.

Martin, who spent two years at Adelsheim, also distinctly felt that he had less than the other children around him. He and his siblings did not wear expensive brand-name clothes. There were days when the portions that his mother served were smaller than usual. Despite the family's struggles, though, Martin and his two sisters never knew hunger. He and his siblings could always go to his grandparents who lived close by to get something to eat.

Martin's childhood was by no means easy. His little sister was sexually abused by his mother's boyfriend. His older sister became addicted to heroin. But in contrast to the American respondents, he can still easily recall happy childhood memories. Martin remembered going on vacation to the Baltic Sea. The German government subsidizes these kinds of trips for families with children as a preventive or rehabilitative measure to address mental and chronic physical health problems of parents and children.[7] This trip was Martin's favorite childhood memory. "We took a boat and when we went for walks, my mom pushed me and my sister around in a little cart. I played a lot with my big sister. She did not want play with cars so we played Barbie."

When I asked him why he believed he ended up in prison, Martin replied without hesitation that he wanted adults to notice him. He committed crimes, such as breaking and entering or drug dealing, to get his mother's attention. As a single mother, she worked a lot and was focused on his two sisters. Martin was the middle child who seemed to function relatively well on his own and he felt overlooked. He believed that receiving more monetary support from the German government could have gone a long way for his family—maybe his mother would have had to work less and could have been more present. According to his case summary file, Martin is emotionally fragile. He has been addicted to drugs and he tried to commit suicide.

At eighteen years old, Jens was the youngest respondent I interviewed in Germany. Jens's grandparents came from Croatia during the 1960s and both his parents were born in Germany. By the time Jens had turned five, he had started living with his grandmother and her second husband. As a little boy, he just wanted to be back with his mother, but she struggled with drug addiction and couldn't take care of him.

Jens described his grandmother as a social climber. In her second marriage she had married "up." Her second husband was ethnically German and, in Jens's recollection, he was a wealthy man. Jens did not like staying with his grandmother and step-grandfather because they were imposing their "bourgeois" values on him. "I had to wear a turtleneck sweater and corduroy pants . . .," he explained. His grandparents did not allow him to listen to hip-hop but forced him to put on classical music. Jens was resentful of his grandmother and what he perceived as her newly acquired "habitus." He insisted that he was of a "different social background." He couldn't just sit at home and study. He wanted to spend time with his friends.

When his grandparents couldn't manage him anymore, he was admitted to a psychiatric hospital. While he was not certain about his exact diagnosis, he remembered doctors telling him he had an attachment disorder and anger problems. After being discharged, he was sent to a boarding school for children with developmental challenges. He did not last long there and moved from one foster home to another. Jens couldn't remember exactly how many different places he was sent to, but he believed that he must have lived in about twenty different homes.

When I interviewed him, he had already spent a year in prison for theft and extortion. Having been institutionalized for most of his teenage years, he insisted that he did not perceive Adelsheim as "punishment." He was bored and wished he could do more sports—for example, weight lifting—like in the US boot camps he had heard about. Jens's biggest worry was that he would start committing crimes again after his release: "If I begin vocational training," he explained, "I'll make eight hundred euros a month; I'll make the same amount of money in a few hours just driving around with my friends."

Arslan faced the longest prison sentence of the German sample. When I met him during the summer of 2017 he had already been locked up for six years in various facilities. Arslan insisted, though, that he had a happy childhood. He felt loved and never lacked anything. Arslan did indeed have plenty of good memories to share. He happily recalled car rides with his father through the snowy streets of Stuttgart. He and his father went sledding at the hilly park surrounding the picturesque Solitude castle. Afterward, they usually went out to eat, drink, and warm themselves up.

Arslan believed that he committed crimes because he wanted to have money to party and buy himself expensive clothes. He was twelve years old when his father died of lung cancer. After that, he spiraled out of control. According to his own assessment, he did not respect or listen to anyone anymore. He mentioned, not without pride, that the police in Stuttgart knew him well and that he was classified as a high-level juvenile offender. At the same time, his mother fell ill and had a heart attack. She was unable to work and the family had to move into government housing. Based on their family size, the government had allocated only a one-bedroom apartment for Arslan's mother and her two youngest sons. Since Arslan was incarcerated when the family had to move, there was no space reserved or him. Arslan felt the social decline intensely. He went from a well-off residential area to an undesirable part of Stuttgart with high-rise apartments. Many of those apartments were occupied by families who had a migration background like Arslan's family. While the neighborhood was clean, with several affordable grocery stores within walking distance and plenty of green space, Arslan and his family knew the difference. In their old lives they were able to afford luxuries like Bosch kitchen utensils. In their new home, they had to content themselves with what the government deemed necessary.

SOCIAL SERVICES IN THE UNITED STATES AND GERMANY

A welfare state, Gøsta Esping-Andersen argued, doesn't just redistribute resource, it engineers a different system of stratification (1990). The entanglement in the German welfare state came at cost: While their peers lived full and self-defined lives, the young men and their families operated within the confines of welfare governance. Their perceived needs—a bigger apartment, for example—may not match the government allocation of square footage for a family, especially when, as in Arslan's case, a family member stayed in the apartment intermittently. Even though their lives were comparatively stable, the respondents' families hovered on the fringes of society. Understandably, the young men judged their own social position in relation to their middle-class peers. While their families struggled, the ethnic German majority around them thrived. Automobile companies like Daimler, Porsche, or Bosch pay high wages even to untrained workers.[8] Before the COVID-19 recession, the booming economy had generated a record tax income for the government.[9] The young men I met were not part of this economic boom, and from their perspective they did not benefit from living in affluent communities. As children they felt the difference between them and the others, mostly ethnic German families, even more intensely because they were a minority left behind by the increasing wealth around them.

The situation of the American young men was in many ways the exact opposite of the German group. In contrast to southern Germany, Central Pennsylvania has been an economically depressed region for many years. Once prosperous towns like Allentown or Bethlehem never recovered from the closing of the steel mills (Gimple 1999). Currently, the area is being ravaged by the opioid epidemic. In 2018, the state government of Pennsylvania reported that 4,422 people had died of a drug overdose that year.[10] With a death rate of 36.1 per one hundred thousand, only three US states—Maryland, Delaware, and West Virginia—have been hit harder.

As I have argued elsewhere (Soyer 2018), the US respondents and their caregivers did not have easy access to any nonpunitive governmental social services. Any other assistance a family might be able to receive had to be cobbled together from temporary government programs and nongovernmental welfare providers, such as food or clothing banks.[11] Navigating a decentralized web of organizations can be challenging, especially for those who are struggling to find steady employment in the first place. The same obstacles—mental or physical health problems—that thwart people's participation in the workforce likely also prevent them from maximizing welfare benefits. Living in segregated neighborhoods and surrounded by poverty, they experienced being poor physically as being hungry or homeless. They were never directly confronted with the comfortable lifestyle afforded to upper-middle-class children (Shedd 2015).

The comparison of both groups emphasizes the relative experience of poverty and punishment. Symbolic interactionists have taught us that we tend to judge our own social experience in relation to those we believe to be our peers (Mead 1967; Hochschild 1989). A much less segregated society than the United States, southern Germany has retained a comparatively broad middle class, even as German society has become more unequal. The young men in Pennsylvania were surrounded by deep-rooted poverty. The kind of wealth and privilege the US upper middle class is able to accumulate was beyond their imagination (Reeves 2017; Khan 2011). The young men did not perceive their exclusion as an anomaly—because they were surrounded by poverty. The "opportunity hoarding" of the upper middle class and the legacy of housing discrimination all but assured that the young men may have lived in proximity to extreme wealth, while their immediate environment was steeped in severe disadvantage (Conley 2009).

The US respondents also narrativized their pathways into crime in terms of the deprivation they grew up in. Their social imagination developed in relation to the segregated neighborhoods they called home. Being remarkably resilient, the young men did not accept their class position but strived for upward mobility within their community (Young 2004). Affiliating themselves with drug dealers was an expression of agency. From a child's perspective, those men were on top in a neighborhood that offered very limited pathways to conventional success (Contreras 2013; Bourgois 1995; MacLeod 1987). The drug dealer's conspicuous consumption was an antidote to the hunger pains, homelessness, and humiliation they experienced growing up.

The German young men had very different childhoods. They were surrounded by prosperity that explicitly excluded them. Armend exemplifies the most extreme case of poverty I encountered in southern Germany. In the context of US public housing units I have visited, though, the family's situation was hardly remarkable. However, in a German social context his family's living conditions were disturbing. Their trailer stood out among the well-maintained, single-family homes prevalent in Armend's hometown.

Blake and Armend grew up under roughly similar socioeconomic circumstances. Both their families relied on government support to make ends meet. Looking at these two families comparatively demonstrates the relative experience of poverty. While Blake said that he was initially oblivious to his family's level of disadvantage, Armend always knew that he was poor. That is family was an anomaly is admitted by the well-to-do residents of the picturesque village he lived in. He felt singled out and he was ashamed of his living quarters. In fact, he disliked staying there so much that he seemed to prefer returning to prison when he violated the conditions of his parole. Subjective levels of discomfort and suffering are difficult to align with the objective disadvantage the young men encountered in both societies. Armend was ashamed of his upbringing and what it represented to his German neighbors. Blake felt better about himself but objectively his family had to struggle harder to get by.

"It could be worse" is not exactly a ringing endorsement of Germany's welfare system. It is important to note, though, that even the most disadvantaged families of the German group were able to preserve a modicum of dignity and stability for their children. The happy childhood memories the German respondents were able recall testify to how meaningful this kind of support had been.

At the same time, the welfare state solidified the young men's outsider status. Arslan, for example, stopped going to the social welfare office that was supposed to help him find employment after he was released from prison. He could not effectively express what exactly kept him away, but he clearly stated that he did not want the government to have any more control over his life. Not engaging with government institutions and following their rules also meant that he was not eligible for support and that his family was going to be less likely to be moved to bigger apartment.

CONCLUSION

In contrast to the benevolent exclusion the German sample lived through, the young men in Pennsylvania experienced brutal marginalization justified by instrumental rational calculations of the market. Since their parents had failed to successfully find their place in a modern workforce, US society felt no obligation to provide for their children. In fact, withholding support has shifted what Francoise Bonnet (2019) has referred to as the "upper limit." Theoretically, incarceration—driven by the principle of "less eligibility"—deters crime and incentivizes participation in the labor force, by being *less desirable* than the life of the lowest paid worker (Rusche and Kirchheimer 2003). The narratives of the young men in Pennsylvania show that this may not be the case anymore. Childhood poverty had created such an unpredictable environment that in some cases prison offered more stability, safety, and social support than life on the outside.

Most recently, Luisa Schneider (2021) has observed a similar tendency in Germany. In her ethnography of homeless individuals in the eastern German city of Leipzig, she noticed that the welfare state in Germany did not reach this population effectively. For the unsheltered men and women, prison offered reprieve from the streets. Being incarcerated was framed as a "vacation," allowing the unhoused to get a regular meal and avoid freezing temperatures during the winter months (4). Schneider's work, more than anything, demonstrates the differences between both countries. In Germany, the welfare state fails to catch a population that, owing to mental illness or drug addiction, cannot overcome the bureaucratic hurdles to receive support. The men and women who live on the streets of Leipzig exist outside the economic incentive structure. From the rather callous perspective of "less eligibility," it is not surprising that their life on the streets is worse than being incarcerated. There is no need to incentivize them to do work since they have "opted out."

In the United States, a very different population faced the "less eligibility" dilemma. The young men and their families did not represent the lowest socioeconomic stratum. Unlike the homeless Schneider observed, their mothers worked at least intermittently. As they moved in with relatives or lived in shelters, families still operated within the regular economy. By and large, the young men's families were part of the working poor that could not make ends meet, even if their mothers and grandmothers worked multiple jobs (Ehrenreich 2001). The homeless in Leipzig may have desired a "vacation" in prison; in Pennsylvania children were forced to realize that prison had more to offer than their neighborhood.[12] As I will show in the following chapter, the cultural dynamics visible in the narratives about their marginalization on the outside also define how the young experienced punishment inside prison.

CHAPTER FOUR

Retribution and Domination

Living through Punishment in Germany and the United States

The juvenile prison in Adelsheim sits at the edge of a pictur-esque southern German town. Dating back to 779, two small cas-tles are a reminder that Adelsheim was once a chiefdom—home to knights whose descendants still bear the town's last name. The Adelsheim prison is the only remaining juvenile prison in Baden-Württemberg. The second such institution was closed down in in 2015 and is now being used as a holding prison for refugees and other immigrants prior to their deportation.[1]

Visitors who enter the JVA Adelsheim do not have to pass through metal detectors or undergo pat downs. The young men are housed in individual cells. A transitionary unit, located on the outskirts of the complex, has the feel of student housing with a shared kitchen and dorm rooms. The daily routine usually leaves very little time for the kind of unstructured lingering I have observed in US prisons. Overlooking the calm scene of young men playing soccer, walking to school or work, it becomes evident why American observers consider Germany a model for humane punishment and successful rehabilitation (Turner and

Travis 2015).[2] After visiting German prisons, researchers from the Vera Institute of Justice shared a video of German penal practices. The caption states: "This is what a prison system looks like when it is centered around treating people humanely."[3]

While these differences in incarceration rates are stark (see chapter 1), they are only one aspect of the complex punishment projects that are executed in both countries. Relying on Durkheim's (1964) understanding of the law as a representation of "collective conscience" (194, 80–81), this chapter challenges the one-dimensional representation of Germany as a safe haven for rehabilitation in comparison to the American justice system.

Synthesizing historical-cultural analysis with observations, as well as the respondents' narratives, I argue that both systems follow a different cultural logic of punishment. The criminal justice system in Germany focuses on establishing cultural hegemony over a population considered to be at odds with core German values of obedience, subordination, and a Christian belief system (Adorno 1950). The programs administered in prison seamlessly connect to social services on the outside and prepare the young men for a life in the lower socioeconomic strata of German society.

In the United States, an individual criminal act is treated as an inexcusable failure to use the wide-ranging economic and cultural freedom that defines the country. Restricting individual freedom for a long period of time may be considered a visceral response of a state, whose capitalist machine has to draw on specific kinds of individualistic rule breaking and innovation to secure continuous growth (Merton 1938; Messner and Rosenfeld 2007).

This chapter reveals how punitive practices are connected to the dominant social and political project of a given society.

Germany's more lenient punitive system ironically grew out of a punitive logic that relied on the complete dehumanization of the other. Today's prisons have retained dehumanizing assumptions about their prisoners even as sentence length and social services adhere to a comparatively more humane rehabilitative ideal.

THE COUNTRY WHERE THE CANNONS BLOOM

I usually begin my undergraduate course on the sociology of punishment by showing a German documentary about prison life. The film markets itself as a perspective on the dangers of being a correctional officer at one of Germany's most notorious high-security prisons—colloquially referred to as Santa Fu (JVA Fuhlsbüttel) in Hamburg.[4] The documentary shows a female correctional officer politely knocking on cell doors while wishing inmates a good morning. Some of the incarcerated men are trained to become cooks and are wielding knives in the kitchen. Their supervisor emphatically states that he trusts his trainees, even if they have committed a violent offense. Finally, during a routine inspection, the interior of a cell comes into view. It looks like a dorm, equipped with light-brown, wooden furniture, a desk, drawers, a bed, and a sink. The camera shows personal kitchen utensils sitting on shelves: a mixer and a juice press, items that are prohibited in American prisons. While the officers talk about how easily simple objects can be fashioned into weapons, they systematically inspect the belongings and are careful to leave the cell as they have found it.

New York students, used to living in shoe-box sized apartments, are usually amazed by the comfortable set up. Some wonder whether Germany goes too far in accommodating violent offenders. What I do not tell them is that Santa Fu was a concentration camp during the Third Reich. Mostly holding political prisoners, it used to be one of the "most notorious terror institutions in National-Socialist Germany."[5]

As a twenty-one-year old intern of a local Hamburg newspaper, I witnessed the long shadow of this terror firsthand. I wrote my first long-form piece about an organization providing care for elderly victims of the National Socialist dictatorship. Tagging along with one of the nurses, I met Karl who had been incarcerated at the concentration camp Santa Fu as a member of the German Communist Party. I tried to ask him about his time there but he did not want to engage with me. His nurse explained to me that he is haunted by his memories. Karl lived in a small room and he was barely able to move without help. He felt trapped; being immobilized brought back traumatic memories. His nurse sometimes stayed for hours when he noticed that his patient was particularly distraught. Karl's speech was slurred but right before I left, he turned to us and asked, "I am not at Santa Fu, am I?"[6] In the twenty years since I met Karl, this generation of survivors has vanished. As the Nazi dictatorship has become a distant historical event, the narrative of Germany as a beacon of rehabilitation and humane punishment has been able to flourish.

The spatial continuity between the former concentration camp and current maximum-security prison in Hamburg is only one of the more obvious indictors that Germany did not radically break with its past. After the Nuremberg trials, the Cold War loomed and the allied forces approached denazification much more pragmatically. The principle of *legal certainty* became part of the German constitution. A basic doctrine of a modern democracy, it was supposed to prevent another dictator from hollowing out the country's legal foundation. At the same time, the notion that what had been considered legal at one point cannot be punished as illegal behavior retroactively protected Nazi perpetrators—who for the most part had acted within the legal parameters of the Third Reich—from being held responsible for their crimes. In 1950, the German government reinstated civil servants with connections to the Nazi regime that had been relieved of their duties in 1945. Among many other occupations (career soldiers, mid-level bureaucrats), judges who had sanctioned Nazi law found themselves again in powerful positions—tasked with rebuilding the judiciary of the newly established Federal Republic of Germany (Eichmüller 2012).[7]

Probably even more consequential in terms of cultural continuity were the many "ordinary men" (Browning 1992), low level SS or Gestapo henchmen, and former Wehrmacht soldiers, who inevitably made up a significant part of postwar German society. As the German army struggled to control the vast territory in Eastern Europe it occupied initially, Wehrmacht soldiers, alongside the SS and former police, were tasked with preventing "partisan" activity. A significant number became complicit in crimes against humanity (Hartmann 2004). Many of those who survived the disastrous invasion of the Soviet Union returned home as broken men. The last thing they wanted was to be held accountable for what they had seen and done.[8]

My grandparents, like many others of this generation, chose instead to focus on rebuilding and remembering the good times—for example, the camaraderie, the way Hitler put German men to work building infrastructure, most notably, the highways. And of course nobody knew about what happened to the Jews. "We thought they were put to work," my grandmother once told me. This avoidance of accountability on the familial level persisted despite—or maybe because—the political leadership consistently professed Germany's guilt on the world stage (Welzer 2002). While the government took over collective responsibility for the Holocaust, the average German was allowed to turn inward and focus on the good things that defined their country before 1933—for example, virtues such as precision and hard work. Other examples of this included German contributions to classic culture, as well as current events—notably, Germany winning the soccer World Cup in 1954 (Schiller 2015).

As the legacy of the atrocities committed during the Third Reich receded further into the background, right-wing political opinions that used to be uttered behind closed doors became socially acceptable again (Walter 2003). The influx of refugees during the mid-2010s has given rise to an anti-immigrant rhetoric resonating beyond right-wing fringe groups. The so-called *Alternative für Deutschland* (AfD), a party explicitly running on a law-and-order, anti-immigrant platform has been elected by a large margin to the state parliament of Baden-Württemberg.

In practice, vilifying immigrants is out of alignment with the reality of the German criminal justice system and steadily declining crime rates (Höynck and Ernst 2014). At the same time, the German criminal justice system is also not as lenient as it seems. Courts can impose indeterminate prison time should someone be deemed too dangerous to be released. From a legal standpoint, this so-called *Sicherungsverwahrung* (preventive detention; see also chapter 1) is not considered a prison sentence anymore and is tied to regular psychological evaluations (Laubenthal 2007). Nevertheless, the affected individuals continue to be housed at a prison facility without a clear understanding of when and even if a release is possible.[9] In 2008, this provision was extended to include persons under the age of twenty-one. It can even be applied post hoc to those sentenced before the law was changed.

The young men I interviewed in Germany grew up in a social climate that became less tolerant of crime and more openly hostile against those who are not ethnically German. Living in a society that rewards conformity and nurtures suspicion toward immigrants unavoidably impacted how the respondents saw themselves and the kind of future they were able to imagine.

Punishment in Southern Germany

The concept of Germany as a culturally and ethnically homogenous country is visible in the daily practices of the prison in Adelsheim. Forty percent of the inmates identify as Muslim. But when I visited the institution for the first time in 2016, the only clerical support available was a priest. During the past years, a part-time imam has been brought on. Prisons in Baden-Württemberg do not offer halal food for Muslim inmates; instead, inmates have the option to eat regular food without pork. Until a few years ago, this kind of food was officially referred to as Moslemkost (muslim food), a term inadvertently evoking Nazi terminology like Judenstern (Star of David) or Judenrat (Jewish Council) (Bartsch et al. 2017).

Children considered ethnically German are in the minority. In 2019, 68 percent of those incarcerated in Adelsheim had a "migration background" (Stelly and Thomas 2021), while only about 18 percent of the male population under twenty-five fall into this category in Baden-Württemberg's general population.[10]

Even though the families of the young men at Adelsheim come from many different countries, letters originating in

Germany have to be written in German to be delivered to their recipients.[11] There is no demographic data available about the officers or counselors working there. However, during the three summers I conducted interviews, the staff I met were overwhelmingly ethnically German. As far as I was able to discern, German was also the language of conversation in all areas of the prison (i.e., work, school, therapy). In its ethnocentric focus, the prison reflected the young men's experience on the outside. Despite increasing immigration, Germany remains a homogenous society. Whether they were in prison or out in the community, those who had a "migration background" were reminded regularly that their cultural heritage was of little value to German society.[12]

Marko, whose family is Roma, experienced his incarceration as a complete deconstruction of his personality. Marko recalled how one of his therapists challenged his beliefs and nullified everything he thought he knew. In retrospect, Marko believed that his therapists' approach enabled him to change in a positive way. He insisted that his self-presentation as a "thug" explained why people may have been prejudiced against him. From his perspective, his "habitus," not other people's racism, was to blame when nobody wanted to hire him before he was incarcerated.

For a majority of the young men their families' welfare dependency amplified their outsider status in the community. Aside from receiving financial and material goods, they also participated in a significant number of therapeutic interventions administered by the German Youth Welfare Office (Jugendamt).[13] Most respondents recalled regular contact with social workers, who visited their families in an attempt to mitigate conflicts between them and their parents. Marcel, one of the few respondents who was ethnically German, for example, had been extensively involved in the German welfare system. His parents divorced when he was a young child and he had very little contact with his father while he was growing up. Marcel and his brother were around eight and nine years old, respectively, when they had to live with a foster family for a month while their mother was hospitalized.[14] His mother continued to struggle with alcoholism. She was overwhelmed with her day-to-day responsibilities and the family remained in an assisted living facility. When Marcel and his brother moved out into their own apartment, the welfare system continued to cover their rent and paid the allotted monthly allowance for their living expenses.

According to Marcel, the welfare system stopped payments because he refused to accept transitionary employment that had been arranged for him. Marcel said that he lacked the credentials to learn a trade or find another lucrative job he would enjoy. Committing crimes therefore seemed the faster and easier route to get money. In his case file Marcel was described as unwilling to work. A social worker observed that his social environment did not encourage a productive life-style. Marcel, his mother, and his brother seemed to spend their days watching TV together, and Marcel could not be motivated to participate in the workforce.

When I asked him what he planned to do after his release, he was uncertain as well. He had decided to max out his sentence. For the first time in his young adult life, he was not going to be under the supervision of a social worker telling him what to do. Marcel was looking forward to not having any government officials meddling with his life. He planned to stay with a friend for a few weeks and hoped to find work at a company that cleans office buildings. Marcel's family represents a more extreme case of welfare dependency, but a majority of the young men's families relied on the social welfare system to cover rent and living expenses.

In prison the young men encountered a more regimented version of the German welfare state (see also chapter 1). Adelsheim offers eighteen apprenticeship programs, such as metal worker, electrician, baker, butcher, and gardener, as well as painter and carpenter.[15] Young men who had finished at least nine years of schooling and passed final examinations were eligible to enroll in job training. In 2014, 68 percent of the young people held at Adelsheim participated in these job training programs. Approximately a third of the remaining 32 percent were enrolled in educational support programs to help them finish the schooling required to become an apprentice (Stelly and Thomas 2017).

In addition to educational programming some young men were allowed to leave prison to participate in recreational activities such as group bike rides or grocery shopping.[16] Once their release date approached, time on the outside became more sustained. To ensure a smooth reentry they were supposed to stay with their families for several days once they had reached the final stretch of their prison time. Since the boundaries between the community and juvenile prison were permeable, the German respondents did not experience the same level of restrictive physical captivity the American respondents recalled. To their own astonishment, some even felt positively connected to their place of confinement.

Arslan, the only respondent who had spent five years there, for example, remembered that he felt at home in his cell. Although he preferred to be with his family, his cell offered a sense of privacy and safety that he enjoyed after visiting his family. Arslan believed that the unit he was assigned to had made it possible for him to settle in. The part of the prison he lived in had a particular focus on psychosocial development. Arslan knew that there was always some psychologist or social worker there he could turn to when he felt down. "It is a real community here," he explained.

In contrast to Arslan, Tyrone resented the therapist he had to speak to. On the other hand, he embraced the structured environment Adelsheim offered. Before his prison stay, he lived in an abandoned house that he shared with other children who lived on the street. He found it difficult to motivate himself to work. As he explained, in prison he could see a clear connection between working, making money, and being able to afford items—mostly food—he desired from the commissary. Having an incentive to work helped him to commit to his daily tasks, and he developed a routine he had not been able to establish on the outside.

It is important to remember that framing incarceration positively is a form of meaning-making—a coping mechanism that allows young men to get through the fundamentally traumatic event of being removed from their family and friends (Soyer 2016). At the same time, none of the German respondents reported the kind of physical segregation and emotional deprivation American respondents recalled when I interviewed them. Given the fluid boundaries between the community and prison life, the German respondents did not experience their incarceration as "social death" (Patterson 1982). They lived, rather, through a more extreme version of the bureaucratic management they had been exposed to already because of their families' dependency on government support.

THE NEW JIM CROW AND THE SPIRIT OF CAPITALISM

The life trajectories of the American respondents have in many ways been impacted by social forces diametrically opposed to the experience of the German group. The young men in Germany grew up poor but the welfare system met their basic needs. Their prison term rarely extended over years and nobody in the German group experienced involuntary homelessness. The young men I encountered at SCI Pine Grove represented a lost generation—old enough to get caught up in mass incarceration and young enough for their childhood to be deeply affected by Bill Clinton's welfare reform (Soyer 2018). Born in the mid to late 1990s, they belong to a generation that was not supposed to face any more discriminatory legal barriers. The civil rights movement had achieved significant legal victories during the 1950s and 1960s; middle-class professions also became more accessible for African Americans during that period (Wilson 1990). The families of the young men I met did not experience this kind of upward mobility. On the contrary, their families' lives were upended when factory jobs disappeared and mass incarceration became one of the defining experiences in segregated, inner-city communities (Garland 2001; Western 2006).

Over the last decade, academic and public discourse has increasingly described the US criminal justice system as a natural extension of the many ways the United States has dehumanized their nonwhite population for centuries. Michelle Alexander's bestselling book *The New Jim Crow*, as well as the countless publications that followed it, reveal how systemic racism has shaped law enforcement, courts, and policy-making (Lopez-Aguado 2018; Van Cleve 2016; Goffman 2014; Rios 2011). Alexander presents mass incarceration of Black bodies as the newest iteration of organized, violent oppression that Black communities have been subjected to since the first slaves arrived on American soil in 1619. Mass incarceration is "The New Jim Crow": Black men are systematically removed from the public sphere and political realm as they are spending decades in prison for minor drug-related offenses.

Understanding the US criminal justice system through the lens of racialized violence has been a necessary corrective. However, by focusing on race as the defining variable of criminal justice involvement, another equally significant element of the US criminal justice system has been sidelined. American prisons do not only disproportionally incarcerate Black and Brown bodies; most of all they remove *poor* Black and Brown bodies from their communities (Muller and Roehrkasse 2022).

Empirical data confirm that criminal justice involvement often co-occurs with poverty-related social problems such as untreated mental illness, drug addiction, low levels of education, and unemployment. According to a Bureau of Justice Statistics (BJS) report, 41 percent of inmates in state prison have not completed high school (Harlow 2003). While being incarcerated decreases the probability of employment after release, a majority of incarcerated people have never been well-integrated in the labor market (Slavinski and Spencer-Suarez 2021; Western 2018). Fifty-six percent of incarcerated persons in the United States reported no annual earnings prior to being in prison. Another 30 percent indicated earnings between five hundred and fifteen thousand dollars (Looney and Turner 2018). Studies also confirm that serious mental illnesses like schizophrenia or bipolar disorder are significantly more prevalent in prisons than in the community (Bronson and Berzofsky 2017; Prins 2014; Teplin et al. 2005).

In a sad and ironic twist of history, the deinstitutionalization of mental health care and the dismantling of welfare state have left today's prisons as the only centralized government institutions reliably providing shelter and food for significant numbers of Americans in mental and economic distress. Loic Wacquant describes the concurrent rise of mass incarceration and the precipitous decline of the welfare state as an interrelated process: "Welfare revamped as workfare and prison stripped of its rehabilitative pretension," he writes in *Punishing the Poor*, "work jointly to invisibilize problem populations—by forcing them off the public aid rolls, on the one side, and holding them under lock, on the other . . ." (2009, 288).

Today's prisons are filled with what Karl Marx once called the Lumpenproletariat: Men and women who are born into poverty and never have a chance to move beyond it. A significant number of these people struggle with mental illness and drug addiction. Many know what hunger feels like and what it means to be homeless. After their release, a majority of them lack the social, cultural, or economic capital to survive independently in a hypercapitalist society (Butterfield 2018; Soyer 2018; Sufrin 2017; Wacquant 2009).

Punishment in Pennsylvania

For the young men I interviewed in the United States incarceration at SCI Pine Grove represented a radical break in their life course. Being sentenced as adults meant that some respondents had decades in prison ahead of them. Issac, who was serving twenty to forty years for murder in the third degree, tried to take a pragmatic approach: "I just want to get it over with, I ain't trying to sit here and think about it and keep thinking about it and drive myself crazy about it. I'm ready to start it and get it over with," he explained. Being locked away for years severed social ties to the outside world. Dylan, who was at the beginning of his decades-long sentence, did not have any regular contact to his family or friends anymore. He speculated that it was not worth it for them to stay in touch with someone whose earliest release date was twenty-five years from now. Dylan remembered that he did a lot for others when he was on the outside. He was not surprised, though, that nobody had tried to stay in touch with him. As Dylan put it, "Everybody forget what you did no matter what it was once you locked up."

For those who had to adjust to many years ahead in the Pennsylvania Department of Corrections the few rehabilitative measures Pine Grove offered were a farce. Robert, who was at the beginning of a fifteen-to-thirty-year sentence for the sale or transfer of stolen firearms, felt that planning for the future was futile. Before his arrest he been interested in working with cars, but thinking about any concrete future employment was pointless: "The world is going to be changed so much. I'm not going to know what's going on. . . . If I try to get back into auto tech I'm going to be so far behind."

Pennsylvania prisons usually offer vocational training in HVAC, carpentry, and custodial maintenance. However, the young men participating in the Young Adult Offender program were not eligible to enroll in these programs since they are reserved for the general adult prison population. The Pennsylvania group received some educational support, such as GED classes, but they did not participate in any job training that could lead directly to employment after their release.

Being incarcerated at SCI Pine Grove had a significant psychological impact on the US respondents. Elijah, who had grown up in the Bronx but was arrested in Pennsylvania for drug trafficking, believed that you had to be "mentally prepared" to live in a prison environment. Even though he spent time at New York City's infamous Rikers Island, being in state prison remained psychologically taxing. It was not always possible for him to do the cognitive work to remain calm. "Like once in two, three months or so, I get that day I wake up, and the only thing that's on my mind is just home," he explained.

Samuel, who had received a two-to-four-year sentence, resorted to sarcasm to mitigate the feeling that he was at the mercy of correctional personnel. He believed that the COs considered him to be a difficult inmate because he smiled a lot. He believed that his smiles indicated to the COs that they were not able to intimidate him. According to Samuel, "they [the COs] do things they think is gonna hurt us. . . . Like to break us down psychologically. And it doesn't bother me. I know at the end of the day who I am, what I do." Remaining detached gave him a feeling of power over a situation in which the cards were stacked against him.

Sending someone to solitary confinement was the ultimate punitive tool to control the young men at SCI Pine Grove. Several respondents reported having been in and out of solitary confinement for months on end. Being sent to the "the hole," as the young men referred to it, meant to be locked up alone for twenty-three hours of the day. Jaxon remembered being sent to solitary confinement several times over the course of his time at Pine Grove. He recalled that his last stint in "the hole" had a deterrent effect on him. He believed that being by himself and having a great deal of time to consider his actions altered his thinking process. He credits his time in solitary confinement for his understanding that his actions have consequences.

Like Jaxon, a majority of the respondents tried find meaning in the many years they had to spend on the inside. Tyrell, for example, appreciate that he was able to learn how to read at Pine Grove. At the same time, he believed that he would not be able to handle coming back to prison again. As he put it, "I'm not gonna say I'm gonna go out in a blaze of glory if I ever come back. I'm just not gonna put myself in the position to come back again cause like here, they control every aspect of your life."

In contrast to the German respondents, the young men at Pine Grove contextualized the physical and psychological burden of incarceration punishment in relation to the traumatic experiences they had lived through before their arrest. The young men I met in Pennsylvania grew up in abject poverty and had to live through physical and psychological abuse (Soyer 2018). The pain they had endured on the outside inadvertently relativized their perspective on being incarcerated. Austin, for example, who was serving a one-to-five-year sentence, insisted that being in prison had been good for him. He believed that he was able to learn more about himself and to assess what brought him to prison in the first place.

Irrespective of how the young men framed being incarcerated, their punishment was not the subtle kind of leveling the German group experienced. The young men in Pine Grove were physically segregated from the outside world. Some had not seen their parents for years and others had lost social ties to their family and friends entirely. At Adelsheim the young men were prepared to accept their existence as second-tier citizens. Teenagers in Pine Grove were removed from the public sphere entirely. Their punishment symbolized retribution for violent crimes they had committed. The reality of their confinement therefore manifested as physical restraint and segregation that were supposed to inflict a level of pain that would deter them from future violence. In the process the young men lost valuable social ties, and most importantly, they remained utterly unprepared for coping with the disadvantage and poverty that would await them again after their release.

CONCLUSION

The respondents' narratives revealed the cultural mechanisms underlying the punitive projects in both countries. In southern Germany, punishment targeted the young men's "deviant behavior" in relation to norms and values of the middle class. Their outsider status manifested most visibly in their "migration background" and their unwillingness to submit to the bureaucratic domination of the welfare state (Weber 1978). Contextualizing the respondents' experiences culturally and historically relativizes Germany's progressive image. The pervasive ideology of German superiority not only predates Hitler's rise to power; it has also never been reckoned with effectively in postwar German society (Karlauf 2019; Eichmüller 2012; Welzer 2002). Historicizing the Nazi regime, on the other hand, has opened doors for a more aggressive anti-immigrant rhetoric. After initial successes at the state level, the AfD has expanded its political reach significantly. Having been elected to the parliament for the second time in 2021 with 10.3 percent of the votes, the party has become a force to be reckoned with in German politics. In 2018, Alexander Gauland, one of the party's national leaders, did not hold back his assessment of Germany's historical achievements. To the applause of his supporters, he declared: "Hitler and the Nazis are just a speck of bird poop in more than 1,000 years of successful German history."[17]

In parallel with these larger social processes, incarceration entrenched the young men's position at the margins of German society. Children who have a "migration background" were vastly overrepresented in the juvenile justice system of Baden-Württemberg. The state government also makes very little effort to accommodate their cultural or religious heritage. On the contrary, the bureaucratic structures of the juvenile justice system project the ideal of Germany as a culturally and ethnically homogenous country.[18] Not unlike the *child savers* at the beginning of the twentieth century in the United States, the juvenile justice system in southern Germany attempts to reconcile the young men to the social position that had been assigned to them (Platt 1977). In this sense, the juvenile justice system does not offer opportunities for a successful reentry, but provides incentives for the young men to accept their existence at the fringes of society.

Comparing the benevolent exclusion of Baden-Württemberg's juvenile justice system with the visceral retribution in Pennsylvania exposes the punitive logic of both countries: German respondents were punished for deviating from the cultural expectation of the homogenous German middle-class. The American group was punished for their families' failure to "pull themselves up by their bootstraps." The young men's punishment reflects the United States' unflinching commitment to capitalism. The United States relies on its population to secure limitless economic growth by taking risks and pushing physical as well as cognitive boundaries (Merton 1938; Prasad 2012). The young men's destructive attempts at self-preservation have no room in this kind of national myth-making. Removing them permanently from the public sphere may therefore be the logical next step.

While this comparison crystallizes the brutality of incarcerating teenagers in the adult criminal justice system, it also shows that the southern German approach does not eliminate inequality. Neither does it address deeply rooted racist assumptions of cultural superiority. The German juvenile justice system may in fact be a cautionary tale for those seeking to end mass incarceration in the United States. Focusing on rehabilitation without addressing the underlying principles of marginalization will likely not yield the kind of fundamental change that is desired.

CHAPTER FIVE

"I wanna be somebody"

Education and Upward Mobility in Germany and the United States

In the fall of 2020, during the second wave of COVID-19, I relocated with my family to the small village in southern Germany I grew up in. My younger daughter was enrolled in first grade and her sister entered fourth grade—the year in which teachers have to make decisions about the kind of academic tracts students will be attending from fifth grade on. In comparison to the United States, southern German schools decide early on who will be going to a vocational school and who will finish twelve years of schooling with the goal of going to university.[1]

Having both my children go the same school I had attended thirty-four years ago was a surreal experience. A lot has changed since my own first day of school, but many fundamental aspects of schooling have also remained the same. The local elementary school has stayed rather homogenous. In both my children's grades there were only a handful of students from immigrant families. Similar to the way things were in my own childhood, parents worked for the automobile industry. The Porsche development center and factory are located two towns over. Bosch and Mercedes are headquartered within a forty-five-minute drive. With an average of 68,000 euros in savings per person, the area continues to be one of the wealthiest parts of an already wealthy state (Münzenmeier 2020, 32).

A small village in southern Germany may not indicate accurately how Germany has transformed over the past forty years. On the other hand, studies conducted at the national level confirm my local impression of stagnation: The educational system in Germany still fails to uplift children who are not ethnically German and who come from lower-class backgrounds. Children who have a migration background continue to be more likely to be selected into the vocational tract (Baumert, Maaz, and Trautwein 2010). The young men I interviewed at Adelsheim had mostly been attending the lowest level of the classic vocational schools—that of the so-called Hauptschule. While these schools used to offer viable pathways to employment, they are now reserved for a small minority of children who face an array of academic and social challenges (Bold 2020).[2] Similar to the American respondents I interviewed, the German participants I engaged with attended substandard schools. They were relegated to educational institutions serving primarily children who are not ethnically German and who come from lower socioeconomic backgrounds.

Focusing on the range of educational achievement in both samples, this chapter reveals the different ways educational institutions affirmed the respondents' outsider status. The young men's narratives also illustrate how education in and outside of prison reproduced stratification according to race and class in Germany and the United States.

THE LEFTOVERS

In Germany young people can be tried as juveniles until they are twenty-one years old. As a result, many of the young men held at the juvenile prison in Adelsheim are eighteen and older. Being, on average, at the cusp of their twenties at the beginning of their sentence, many have had a long history of failing in school.[3] In 2020, 38 percent of those incarcerated at Adelsheim had finished school with the so-called *Hauptschulabschluss*. This degree has become so marginalized that is not even issued anymore outside special education settings. A majority, about 55 percent, had not even been able to achieve this remedial level of education (Stelly and Thomas 2021).

Among his low-achieving peers in prison, Eren was an exception. The twenty-one-year-old had been at Adelsheim for just over ten months when I interviewed him for the first time during the summer of 2017. On the outside, Eren had been on track to become the first member of his family to enter the Gymnasium. Eren's grandfather had immigrated to Germany from eastern Turkey to work. Eren's father followed him when he was old enough to find more lucrative employment as well. He returned to Turkey to get married and the family relocated to southern Germany permanently afterward. Like the majority of children who have a migration background, Eren was originally sent to vocational school. Defying the odds, he did comparatively well there. One of his teachers noticed Eren's academic ability and encouraged him to aim for continuing his education past the obligatory ten years of schooling.

The encouragement absurdly symbolized how children like Eren tend to be stigmatized in the German educational system. According to Eren, his teacher told him, "You need to work hard, or you just gonna be another one of these 'shitty Kanaken.'" The term "Kanake" refers to people of Arab or Turkish origin. Calling someone a "Kanake" implies that this person is lacking sophistication and intelligence. Unless it is used self-referentially, the term is an insult.

Eren did not care much about being labeled and was simply grateful that his teacher believed in him. He was very motivated initially, but his commitment faltered in part because his family was unsupportive of his educational goals. Eren's father struggled with a gambling addiction and spent the family's money on slot machines. His mother was helpless in the face of her husband's self-destructive habit. Eren remembered that his father was withdrawn. Gambling encompassed his whole existence, and even when he was home, he barely noticed his son. Unsupervised and trying to get away from his family's dysfunction, Eren was drawn to the streets. His attempt to become the first person in his family to graduate high school came to an end when he was arrested on his second day of school for armed robbery.

In prison Eren's options for furthering his education were very limited. When I interviewed him, he was in the process of finishing vocational training as a metal worker. While this type of education could offer a path to a middle-class life, he still had a long way to go. Two years of training and schooling in prison would have to be followed by eighteen months of education and job training on the outside. Only then would he be allowed to call himself a certified metal worker. In the meantime, Eren had disengaged from the idea of ever enrolling at a university. While he likely could have achieved much more under different circumstances, he made good use of his time in prison. As one of the few young men that had finished ten years of schooling successfully, he was able to begin vocational training during his incarceration. As an apprentice he made progress toward a tangible trade that could lead to well-paying employment on the outside. The approximately 55 percent of the incarcerated persons were at Adelsheim without any educational credentials had to take remedial classes before they could even think about starting an apprenticeship.

Armend was one of those young men who were not ready to meet the fairly high standards for enrolling in vocational training. At nineteen years old, he had finished the minimum level of nine years of schooling in prison. Armend spent the remainder of his sentence working in the storage facility of the prison—packing and labeling items. Having been diagnosed with ADHD, and struggling in school all his life, he was proud to have received a degree. He was aware of his limitations and did not aspire to be trained as an apprentice. Instead, the nineteen-year-old envisioned working as an untrained laborer in a storage facility on the outside as well. His greatest ambition was to become a forklift driver.

The reality he encountered on the outside undercut even his modest expectations. Against the advice of his probation officer, Armend went back to live with his family in a small, picturesque village in a tourist area known as the Swabian Alps. In contrast to the rest of the village, the government housing the family lived in was extremely run down and filthy. The family shared the shed-like dwelling with other welfare recipients. One of them openly displayed neo-Nazi tattoos, which intimidated Armend's family. His parents had come to Germany during the war in Kosovo at the end of the 1990s. His mother barely spoke German, and the whole family was marked as being "foreigners" (*Ausländer*) in the very homogenous, small town they lived in.

Armend was stuck at home for most of the day. The social workers in prison had been unable to set him up with a job before he left prison. The degree he had been so proud of was not good enough to secure full-time employment. He had only been able to get an internship at a nursing home, where he did not enjoy working at all. After showing up drunk one morning he never returned.

During the summer of 2018, one year after I had interviewed Armend in prison, he was waiting to be sent back there. Without going into any details, he stated that he had been caught stealing thirty euros. Struggling with depression and alcoholism, and being ashamed of where he lived, he admitted that he was actually looking forward to going back to Adelsheim. While he hoped that this would offer another opportunity for him to change, he was also fatalistic about his future. He seemed to believe that he was never going to be able to live a productive life. At nineteen years old, Armend was set up to become a lifelong welfare recipient.

Achim had achieved the same educational credentials Armend had. Like Armend, he had also been diagnosed with ADHD. Growing up near Heidelberg—a city popular with international tourists—school had never been easy for him. Achim hated doing homework, and he admitted that he was distracted by girls and drugs as a teenager. In contrast to Armend, Achim had several advantages working in his favor after he was released from prison. His parents were embedded in the community they lived in. They owned a house and were gainfully employed. Achim remembered that his family struggled financially when he was growing up, but when I visited them, they seemed established. Owning property in this highly desirable part of Germany, they had achieved a significant level of financial stability. Achim also had light skin and looked ethnically German. Only his father's family had a "migration background." His uncle already worked as a baker, and he helped Achim to secure an apprenticeship at the same bakery.

Becoming a baker has been one of the few options left for people who have only finished minimal schooling. The undesirable working hours and low pay have led to a shortage of apprentices willing to learn the trade. Having the support of his uncle, as well as choosing a trade in need of apprentices, allowed him to enter the labor market successfully after prison.

Achim still struggled with the demands put on him: He had to get up at 4:00 a.m. In addition to learning the craft of baking, he also had to attend school. His supervisor was unhappy with his school performance because he received a C for the practical tasks he was graded on. Nevertheless, Achim was hopeful that he could finish his education and become a baker specializing in making cakes.

During our final interview in the summer of 2019, Achim explained that he had switched to a different trade. In addition to the low pay—he had only received about 340 euros a month after taxes—he had run into personal problems with his supervisor. In the end, he felt it was best to avoid further escalating a conflict. His mother advised him to leave rather than being fired. She also helped him to find a new apprenticeship almost immediately after he quit the bakery. Within a week Achim had started an apprenticeship to become a construction worker. When we spoke, he had just finished his first year as a trainee. This time he had struggled with the theoretical part of his required schooling. He failed his first year, but since he was doing well in the practical aspects of his education, he was able to move forward to year two.

While Achim's path was by no means an easy one, he could rely on his mother's support to help him navigate the complexities of the German apprenticeship system. As a native German, and herself being embedded in the labor market, Achim's mother had distinct advantages over Armend's family. Being able to draw on social connections allowed Achim to overcome the disadvantage of a substandard degree. Being knowledgeable about the kind of apprenticeships that were available further allowed him to adjust his expectations and to make choices that maximized his position in the labor market. Comparing Achim's position to Eren's and Armend's, the advantage of community embeddedness is obvious. Eren and Achim were on similar educational pathways. While Eren labored below his abilities, Achim was exceeding the limitations of his degree. Armend, on the other hand, lacked any social or cultural capital. Unlike Achim, he was not able to build on the educational degree he had achieved while he was incarcerated.

All three cases exemplify the credentialism of German labor market. While the apprenticeship system offers a viable path to a middle-class lifestyle outside a college degree, the requirements are too high for those who suffer from cognitive deficits and are not socially embedded in the community they live in (Haasler 2020).[4] As Eren's example shows, even high-performing students are stereotyped. Additionally, being in prison forced Eren to lower his educational aspirations significantly. Mirroring the quantitative data about schooling in Germany, the three cases demonstrate how the highly selective system affirms the current class structure rather than enabling upward mobility. In the case of Armend and Eren, their "migration background," coupled with their criminal record and challenging family history, all but assured that they were unable to use the German educational system as a path to upward mobility.

"OPPORTUNITIES, THEY'RE NOT GIVEN. YOU GOTTA TAKE 'EM."

Jesus grew up in grew up in Kensington, Philadelphia—a neighborhood the *New York Times Magazine* has dubbed the "largest open-air narcotics market" in the United States.[5] Jesus remembers being surrounded by heroin addicts and drug dealers growing up. Looking up to the dealers and their conspicuous consumption, he believed a lot of children in his neighborhood shared a similar mindset: "I'm not staying poor. I'm not walking to school. Like I want a car. I want a dirt bike. I want a four-wheeler. My mom need groceries. I don't wanna see her crying no more; let me change something."

Jesus was enrolled a segregated elementary school. Based on the latest data from the Philadelphia school district, 84 percent of the students at his former school are considered low-income. Almost 80 percent of the student body identify as Latino. The school is rated two out of ten, and students perform significantly below the state average in reading, math, and science.[6] Jesus went there in the early 2000s. He remembers being a good student and finishing his work more quickly than the others. He does not remember being offered any extra work. Instead, the teachers called his grandmother to pick him up early when there was nothing more to do for him. Even though he was bored and disruptive in school, Jesus always had high aspirations: "Probably like at nine years old . . . I wanted a job, but I wanted to be like one of the Fortune 500 company dudes."

Becoming a drug dealer was the next logical step for him to make a lot of money quickly. School was an afterthought during these years. None of his teachers noticed that Jesus was a gifted student until he entered a juvenile placement center in his midteens. There he was able to finish his GED quickly at the facility and began studying for the SAT. Jesus scored high on the exam without much effort, and his counselor seemed to be amazed. He recalled: "They thought I was gonna be that one kid that came from nothing [and made it]." After his release, he received a scholarship to enroll at Temple University. He started the semester with high aspirations, wanting to become a counselor or psychiatrist, but his enthusiasm waned quickly. Believing he still had time to take college seriously, he became involved in street life again, was rearrested, and ended up dropping out of college. Gambling away the opportunity of a free college education is one of his biggest regrets. As he put it: "Now I'm like alright that shit wasn't worth it."

When I interviewed him in prison for the last time, he was worried about what his future might look like. "Opportunities," he insisted, "they're not given. You gotta take 'em." He knew that his felony conviction was going to make it a lot harder to find those "opportunities." College was not out of the question for him. Like many young men I spoke to, Jesus held on to ideas of entrepreneurship. He envisioned himself as a successful mortician. Maybe, he thought, he could run his own funeral home. He had heard that few people were interested in this kind of morbid work but the need for funerals will always be there. He estimated that he would be able to make about three hundred thousand dollars a year, depending on where he lived and how popular his business would be.

Jesus was the only one in the American sample that had been able to attend a four-year college. Most respondents had not finished high school. If they attended school, they went there to meet friends and not to learn.

Growing up as an African American boy in Philadelphia, Bryan also attended under resourced, segregated schools. Asked about his elementary school years, Bryan bluntly stated: "It sucked. . . . I used to get teased, like they'd call me names, stuff like that." Bryan also remembered being a difficult student. One of his earliest memories was kicking his elementary school teacher in the knee. He recalled that he "was always in detention, always getting suspended." Reflecting on his upbringing, Bryan believed that he took his anger about his father's abuse out on the teachers. Bryan didn't remember any teachers reaching out to help him, and he believed that the teachers at his school in Philadelphia "didn't really care." His teachers would kick him out of class even though it was others who bullied him. When I asked him why the teachers did not stand up to his classmates, he replied: "What can they do? Teachers are scared."

Bryan was even more upset that his teachers looked the other way when it came to his father's domestic violence. His father regularly beat him, and Bryan was certain that the teachers must have known about this: "Teachers can see the scars. They see why I come to school angry every day." Some days he did not want to go home and stayed in school longer voluntarily in order to do extra work. Like Jesus, Bryan was not challenged adequately academically. He remembered getting his work done quickly and then just sitting around being bored. As he got older, "girls, money, and drugs" became more interesting than school. He still wanted to be a good student to make his mother proud, but being on the street gave him much more satisfaction. He remembered thinking: "I'm gonna do what makes me happy."

Miguel, who is s Latino, grew up in Allentown, a mid-sized town that used to be home to the headquarters of Bethlehem Steel. Miguel did not even want to attend school in order to socialize. He avoided going "at all costs" because he was ashamed of being poor and was worried about not fitting in. He had painful memories of other students teasing him: "I was kind of fat and, ugh, I never had clothes that fit me right. So they used to always make fun of me and stuff, and give me a hard time at school." He was certain that teachers and his classmates lived much better lives then he did and looked down on him. When I asked him how he knew that his classmates' lives were so much better than his, he replied: "They're always around wearing better clothes, smiling all the time, having fun, talking about stuff they did or, 'oh, my mom did this'; 'my dad did that.'"

Miguel's mother was an abusive alcoholic who struggled with bipolar disorder. His father was addicted to drugs and paid little attention to his son. Since his mother usually called his father when Miguel caused problems in school, Miguel figured that misbehaving in school would get his father's attention. Miguel also didn't receive a continuous education before his incarceration. His residential instability led him to switch schools so many times he could barely recall when he went where: "I think I went to like five different middle schools and . . . I think I went to about four different elementary schools from moving around too much," he explained.

By the time Miguel was supposed to attend high school, he was homeless and stayed with whomever offered him a couch to sleep on. Miguel lived by himself by the time he was fifteen. Nobody paid attention to whether or not he actually attended school. As Miguel recalled, "Whenever I didn't feel like going to school, I didn't go to school . . . . No one's telling me I have to go; I ended up not going." Miguel did sneak into school from time to time, though, to eat lunch and to see friends even after he stopped officially attending.

Miguel remembered several teachers, counselors, and even some principals trying to help him. In the end, individual attempts could not counterbalance the fundamental instability of his living conditions. He also believed that he was too young to understand the importance of schooling. Similar to other young men I interviewed, Miguel could not utilize schooling as a way out of poverty. His disruptive behavior alienated him from any support the social institution might have offered him. From an early age his interactions with school as an institution were shaped by shame and alienation. Moving from place to place disrupted his education even further (Desmond 2016). He never even attended a school long enough to receive a sustained education or to create lasting social ties to counselors or teachers that could have sustained him in the absence of his parents.

EDUCATION IN GERMANY AND THE UNITED STATES

In both countries, schools have become a battleground for social problems and cultural conflicts. In Germany, educational institutions are supposed to do the work of integration and assimilation. For over twenty years legal and cultural debates have been fought over whether or not female teachers who are Muslims are allowed to wear headscarves in schools.[7] Religious education continues to be part of the curriculum. At the elementary school my children attended during the fall of 2020, it was possible to opt out of the Protestant or Catholic religious instruction, but students who chose not to attend religion classes were dismissed two hours earlier on Fridays. The dismissal time naturally encouraged parents to enroll their children in one form or another of religious education. In Baden-Württemberg schools are only required to offer alternative religious instruction if there are more than eight students at a school who identify with a specific religion.[8]

The German dual educational system has been lauded for offering viable pathways to employment that do not require a college diploma (Jacoby 2014). This praise overlooks the fact that the system's credentialism excludes low achievers like the children who were housed at JVA Adelsheim. Low-achieving students who are not ready to qualify for vocational training are enrolled in so-called prevocational programs. Nationwide, about a third of these prevocational students have refugee status or a migration background. Over the course of three years, only 70 percent of all participants across Germany were able reach the level required to begin an official apprenticeship (Haasler 2021).[9] This leaves 30 percent of those lowest achievers permanently unable to qualify for any work other than being an untrained laborer.

As a significant number of students are left behind, the most academically rigorous schools have become the most popular school choice for the middle and upper middle class. The year I graduated fourth grade in 1990, only 32 percent of fourth graders in Baden-Württemberg were sent to the Gymnasium. During the school year 2019–20, this number rose to approximately 43 percent. Receiving a Gymnasium education remained a middle-class privilege regardless. Children of parents who have a higher level of education are more likely to be send to the most academically rigorous school, preparing them for university attendance (Gil-Hernandez 2019). In 2012 and 2013, 68 percent of the parents who sent their children to the most academically rigorous school, had attended the Gymnasium themselves. Only 4.6 percent of the parents had stopped their education after the mandatory nine years (Kränzler and Cramer 2020). Class and immigrant status overlap significantly as well. According to Diehl and Granato (2018), the intergenerational upward mobility of immigrants in Germany has stagnated. Likely because of marriage migration, the number of Turkish immigrant women who do not hold any educational degree at all was 49 percent in 2012 as opposed to 33 percent in 2000. Being a naturalized citizen has also not significantly impacted educational achievement, especially for students coming from Turkish immigrant families. Finishing the most basic level of schooling (Hauptschule) still remained the most common educational outcome for these children. While those with Turkish roots fare worse than other immigrant groups, likely because of the comparatively low level of parental education, all children from immigrant backgrounds—irrespective of their citizenship status—lag behind their ethnically German peers. In 2018, only 21 percent of all eight graders who had a migration background were enrolled in the academically most challenging schools. The great majority (about 80 percent) of students who are not ethnically German attended school types that do not offer a pathway to higher education (Kränzler and Cramer 2020).

In comparison to Germany, the United States is much less focused on government-mandated credentials. It is not necessary to finish three years of training and schooling to work as a baker or car mechanic. On the other hand, having a high school diploma is an absolute necessity for securing gainful employment. High school drop-outs in the United States are more likely to be unemployed than high school graduates. If they find work, they tend to get paid lower salaries than those who have a high school diploma in hand (McCaul et al. 1992; McFarland, Rathbun, and Holmes 2018). Given that there are only two viable credentials in the United States—a high school diploma or GED—a lot more people in the United States finish high school and become eligible for enrolling in college than in Germany. Of the 2018 cohort in Pennsylvania, 85.8, on average, graduated from high school. This seemingly high number obscures the fact that—similar to Germany—minorities in the United States are disadvantaged when it comes to accessing high-quality education. African American and Latino students are more likely to attend underfunded schools with low graduation rates in high crime neighborhoods (Shedd 2015). Violence in the surrounding neighborhood inevitably has a negative impact on grades and standardized test scores (Burdick-Will 2016; Pelletier and Manna 2017).

In Pennsylvania and most other states, schools are paid for by property tax revenue. Segregated wealthy white neighborhoods, where parents pay high property taxes, are therefore more likely to offer high-quality schooling. Those schools tend to be filled with students from well-to-do, highly educated families. While students of all achievement levels theoretically attend the same school, students from upper-middle-class families have a significantly different experience from students living in poor neighborhoods (Pattillo 1999; Reeves 2017; Owens 2020). Underfunded and underperforming schools are predominantly located in Latino or African American neighborhoods. These schools attend to students who struggle with food insecurity, trauma, and untreated mental health problems. Parents at those schools are also more likely to be involved in the criminal justice system (Haskins 2017; Poole et al. 2021).

Given the complex social problems of the student body, schools in disadvantaged neighborhoods have to offer social services that are not part of their core educational mission. Schools buildings across the United States, for example, continue to be open for lunch during summer break to serve students who face food insecurity. To counter chronic absenteeism, some schools have also added washing machines on site to give students who are ashamed of going to school in dirty clothes places to do their laundry.[10]

The cases discussed in this chapter demonstrate the limitations of administering social services in a school setting. The support provided in schools may not even reach the students that need to be helped most urgently. In Miguel's case, for example, residential instability prevented him from going to school at all. Most importantly, while schools serving low-income students are more involved in offerings social services, they have also become more intimately connected with the juvenile justice system. Researchers have coined the term "school-to-prison pipeline" to describe disciplinary practices in schools mimicking the "zero-tolerance" approach of the criminal justice system. Akin to a classic understanding of deterrence, suspension and expulsion are supposed to prevent perceived disruptive behavior (Hirschfeld 2008). Studies have also consistently shown that Latino and African American students are subjected to harsher and exclusionary punishments in comparison to their white peers for comparable infractions (Skiba et al 2011; Morris 2016; Wegman and Smith 2019). Similar to Bryan and Jesus, many of the respondents I spoke to acted out in school and were eventually expelled. Expulsion solved a problem for the teachers and other students in the classroom, but it removed other teenagers—those represented in this book, for example—even more fully from conventional pathways to success.

CONCLUSION

Jesus, Bryan, and Miguel fell through the cracks of a segregated educational system that was overwhelmed with the social problems of their student body. Like any kindergartners, Bryan, Jesus, and Miguel were probably eager to be in a classroom initially. Learning became secondary as they had to cope with neighborhood violence, drug addiction, domestic abuse, and residential instability.

Even schools in wealthy districts would have had difficulties providing the numerous social services their families needed. The schools most of the young men attended were not well-funded at all. Being located in areas of concentrated poverty, these institutions lacked the resources to address the multitude of social problems their student bodies coped with. In the end, the young men I interviewed were just several among many struggling with difficult home lives. Being disruptive and violent in school alienated Bryan, Jesus, and Miguel even more from the one institution that could have offered them a way out of the cycle of poverty that had engulfed their families for generations (Soyer 2018).

While a majority of the German respondents weren't academically ready to engage in vocational training, the American respondents did not even have the option to build skills useful for finding employment outside prison. For many, being held at SCI Pine Grove was merely a prelude to a longer sentence to be served at another state prison, where they might become eligible for educational programs. In contrast to the German sample, the American respondents did have a path to getting a college education. Given the job market barriers the formerly incarcerated face, attending a community college may even have been a more reasonable goal than finding employment (Pager 2003). The German juvenile prison simply did not offer classes at the educational level needed for university attendance. In practice the possibility of receiving a college education was irrelevant for the young men I met in Pennsylvania as well. None of them considered a college education as a viable option.

The difference between both samples most clearly manifests itself in the young men's hopes and dreams for their future. In the absence of institutional pathways to success, several American participants subscribed to a vague idea of entrepreneurship. This allowed them to maintain the illusion of agency while they were in a holding pattern, waiting to be transferred to another institution (Soyer 2016). German participants who were unable to get an apprenticeship focused on a specific skill like forklift driving. The German young men had already leveled their expectations, while the young men at SCI Pine Grove seemed to hold out hope that the "American Dream" of upward mobility and the attainment of property could still become a reality for them (ibid.). In the end, optimism was difficult to sustain for both samples. Even as they expressed hopes for a better future, past experiences had shown them how difficult it would be to live a successful and engaged life. From an early age, they had experienced educational institutions as place of shame, failure, and punishment. Rejected by the quintessentially middle-class institution, they struggled to imagine a life course that could lead to financial security and emotional stability.

Despite remarkable differences between both educational systems, outcomes were astonishingly similar. In Germany schooling is based on an early selection process that concentrates disadvantaged children who are not ethnically Germany in schools that do not offer a viable pathway into the middle class. The US educational system seems to be less exclusive than the German one. Students of all achievement levels attend the same school. However, the American system is segregated and stratified by race and class as well. Students of color, like children who have a "migration background" in Germany, receive the short end of the stick. In both countries, education does not allow disadvantaged children to catch up to their middle- and upper-middle-class peers (Raudenbush and Eschmann 2015). On the contrary, their educational experience is alienating and pushes them further away from middle-class success. Even students like Jesus or Eren, who could have been high-achieving, experienced schooling as a string of failures

Turning away from school and focusing on what Bryan referred to as "having fun" was a coping mechanism that almost perfectly fits Albert Cohen's (1955) assumptions about a deviant subculture as well as Paul Willis's (1977) famous argument about working-class culture in the United Kingdom. Not fitting into, and eventually being completely excluded from, middle-class institutions encourages young men in both countries to find validation elsewhere—in a subculture that allows them to feel that they have self-worth even if they look and act differently from their middle-class peers.

Final Thoughts

What Price Are We Willing to Pay
for a More Equal Society?

I have used Durkheim's distinction between organic and mechanical solidarity as a starting point to assess the structural and cultural difference between the punitive regimes in Germany and the United States. Durkheim proposed that heterogenous societies, interconnected through the division of labor, operate according to the principles of "organic solidarity." Those more "advanced" societies, Durkheim believed, were more tolerant of differences and therefore less punitive (1964, 112. Homogenous and less developed communities, he argued, are organized according to mechanical solidarity. These societies punish harshly because difference is perceived as a threat to their core functioning (1964, 108). Building on the tension between empirical reality and theory, *The Price of Freedom* has focused on the social institutions and cultural assumptions that define what it means to be an "outsider" in both countries.

Contrary to Durkheim's argument, Germany, the country with lenient punishment structures, is connected by a "solidarity of likeness." Only those who are ethnically German truly belong (Plamper 2019; Brinkmann and Panreck 2019). First, second- and third-generation immigrants are overrepresented in the prison system, as their families have hovered on the margins of German society for decades.

The United States, a more diverse society, is connected by the common goal of economic success (Messner and Rosenfeld 2007; Merton 1938). Even though the country should be a poster child for Durkheimian "organic solidarity," punitive structures have remained retributive. Mass incarceration has filled US prisons disproportionately with men and women from disadvantaged African American or Latino communities (Alexander 2010). Race and class intersect to uphold social boundaries, especially for those who fail to succeed in a hypercapitalist market place (Muller and Roehrkasse 2022). A majority of the incarcerated population never has the opportunity to develop the kind of skills that would allow them to build a middle-class life (Contreras 2013).

Comparing welfare governance and the educational system in both countries shows how current processes of exclusion emerge from social institutions that are supposed to open up opportunities for upward mobility. Being embedded in these institutions, the young men I interviewed developed a culturally specific understanding of their marginalization. Poverty, for example, was a relative experience. The German and American respondents measured their own social status in relation to their peers (Hochschild 1989). As Carla Shedd (2015) has observed, young men who never left their segregated Chicago neighborhoods did not perceive their disadvantage in relation to middle-class white society. Similarly, the respondents I met in Pennsylvania judged their own upbringing in relation to their immediate social environment. Everyone around them was struggling and many had even less than their families did. The German young men, by contrast, contextualized their socioeconomic status in terms of the middle-class and upper-middle-class families that lived around them. Even though the welfare state sheltered them from abject poverty, they felt intensely marginalized. The German welfare system also prevented the kind of traumatic childhood experiences haunting the US sample (Soyer 2018). Unlike the American group, the young men I interviewed in Germany did not have to endure hunger and homelessness. They were able to recall happy childhood memories.

Embeddedness in a social safety net shaped how the respondents narrativized their pathways into crime. As they looked back, the German respondents explained their juvenile offending in terms of psychological burdens caused by the lack of attention, familial tragedies, and dysfunctions. The American respondents, on the other hand, recalled originally resorting to criminal behavior to provide for their families' basic needs. The young men incarcerated in Pennsylvania had lived through an excess of suffering during their childhood. The material and emotional hardships they endured were extreme and provided the backdrop for the abuse and dysfunction they witnessed as children (Soyer 2018).

The attenuating properties of the welfare state also impacted the German sample's experience of incarceration. Again, the German group judged their incarceration in relation to their lives on the outside. Welfare governance had oddly prepared them for their prison stay. The social services on the inside seamlessly connected to the kinds of services they had been exposed to from early childhood on. Incarceration simply elevated the disciplining framework of the welfare state to a new level. Although the boundaries between inside and outside were more permeable in the southern German juvenile justice system than in Pennsylvania, the young men still experienced incarceration as punishment. Even in a juvenile justice system bending toward rehabilitation and social service provision, incarceration remained a punitive experience at its core (Mead 1918; Zimring 2005).

The trauma of abject poverty, on the other hand, clouded the American group's perspective on incarceration. The principle of "less eligibility"—the assumption that conditions in prisons need to be worse than living standards of the lowest-paid workers—did not reflect the experiences of the US sample (Rusche and Kirchheimer 2003; Bonnet 2018). Despite the popular narrative of mass incarceration erasing rehabilitation, rehabilitative measures have persisted (Phelps 2011). In the absence of a comprehensive welfare state, programs offered in prison turn into a convenient disciplinary tool to manage populations desperately in need of such services (Sufrin 2017; Edin and Shaefer 2015; Wacquant 2009; Piven and Cloward 1993). Group therapy and education in prison build skills, but they also keep incarcerated persons occupied. As the failed experiment of Eastern State Penitentiary has shown, isolation and "contemplation" are not feasible logistically, emotionally, and economically (Rothman 2008; Rubin 2021). Putting people to work—even if it is "busy work"—and offering emotional support in group therapy sessions ultimately make prisons run more smoothly. These things provide incentives for good behavior and they create a safer work environment for correctional personnel. As an unintended consequence of the severe deprivation the young men in the United States had lived through, some of them experienced prison as an opportunity to stabilize their life (Soyer 2016; Soyer 2018).

Finally, comparing the educational systems in both societies and their intersection with incarceration contrasts overt exclusion in the United States with subtle leveling in Germany: The interviews in Germany highlighted the strength of the German apprenticeship system. This allowed the incarcerated teenagers to conceive concrete career goals rather than holding on to the vague idea of "finding a job." On the other hand, the narratives also emphasized important shortcomings of the German system: Those who struggle with the most remedial form of schooling—as a majority of the Adelsheim respondents did—have difficulties finding an apprenticeship. The German participants were relegated to manual labor and, in consequence, to low-paying professions. Their educational deficits were often so large that it was impossible for them to find the kind of employment that would secure a comfortable middle-class lifestyle.

Almost paradoxically, while someone who has been recently released from prison in the United States may struggle to find gainful employment (Pager 2003), his or her opportunities to attain a four-year college degree are better than for a young person in Germany tracked into vocational training. Obtaining a GED offers a clear path to community college and eventually a four-year degree. While the community college pathway to a college degree may be shaped by resource scarcity, community colleges can open doors to higher education, especially for economically disadvantaged students of color (Goldrick-Rab 2010).

The common denominator of both groups was their entrenched outsider status. They did not measure up to the behavioral and occupational standards of the middle and upper middle class, and they faced an uphill battle trying to become self-sufficient members of their societies.

BECOMING A MORE EQUAL SOCIETY

Based on the assumptions of Germany as a homogenous community, Germans expects minorities to embrace a so-called German virtues and cultural practices. Yet, despite their best efforts these perpetual immigrants will never be considered part of the German Volk. Their presence is tolerated, but not welcome. Taking this kind of approach to the integration of newcomers would be unthinkable in the United States. For all its history of racism and discrimination against immigrants, the United States embraces—at least in theory—the coexistence of different ideologies and cultural traditions. Rather than emulating homogenous European countries, the United States therefore needs to provide for disadvantaged populations in ways that respects the country's cultural heterogeneity.

Creating a more just society does not entail ending mass incarceration but it also has to include reconceptualizing the welfare state. For a population that struggles to find work, the current welfare policies of incentivizing employment ring hollow. To enter the labor market successfully, people first need to have a stable place to live. Likewise, worrying about putting food on the table or having access to transportation is not conducive to prioritizing long-term goals (Desmond 2016). To curb the permanent crisis pervading the lives of the most disadvantaged families, resources need to be redistributed effectively (Edin and Shaefer 2015). Rather than going to extreme ends to distance themselves from the social problems haunting the poor, those who have profited from inherited advantage need to start sharing institutional and financial resources (Reeves 2017).

In the spirit of serious economic redistribution, unconditional cash transfers could supplement the current patchwork of in-kind support usually provided by local nonprofits. In-cash distributions require complex policy considerations that need to be weighed carefully, but the evidence for their positive impact is unequivocal (Sun et al. 2021.) At the beginning of the twentieth century cash transfers did significantly increase the life expectancy of children (Aizer et al. 2016). Most recently, the COVID-19 pandemic offered the latest test case for board nonstigmatizing, no-strings attached distribution of monetary support. Generous stimulus payment averted what could have easily turned into a humanitarian crisis. The expanded child tax credit lifted children out of poverty. These payments allowed parents to care for their children with dignity while managing an unpredictable pandemic (Hamilton et al. 2021).

Finally, to create a more equal society, both countries have to reframe their ideas about belonging and deservedness. Germany, in particular, has to confront how its self-understanding of a homogenous country impacts stratification. Subtle leveling of those who are not ethnically German has skewed the allocation of resources and systematically alienated immigrants from the center of society. To truly defy their history, Germans need embrace the coexistence of different cultural traditions within their borders. The incessant labeling of second- and third-generation immigrants as non-Germans, their overrepresentation in the criminal and juvenile justice system, and their educational marginalization have to be addressed top-down, both politically and legally.

The policy suggestions I have offered in these last few pages are necessarily vague. I have no illusions about how difficult it is to change social practices that are deeply embedded in a country's national identity. Social change requires social action, but—to end with Max Weber's famous statement—it is "ideas" that have, "like switchmen, determined the tracks along which action has been pushed by the dynamics of interest" (Weber 1946, 280; Lizardo and Stoltz 2018). Comparing Germany and the United States shows how ideas about deservedness, belonging, and worth shape social institutions and, by extension, the self-understanding of those embedded in them. To move beyond well-established mechanisms of "othering," both countries need to stop defining those who struggle as "defective," as lacking the right skin color, work ethic, resilience, or grit. The United States and Germany need to consider the cultural frames and resulting practices that have systematically marginalized those who do not embody the norms and values of the ruling class that has been in power for generations (Erickson 1966).

BEING "A STRANGER" AS METHODOLOGICAL PRACTICE

During my mid-twenties, I spent two years in Israel at the Hebrew University. I went there in 2004 as journalist to get the kind of credentials that would allow me to write about Israeli politics and German-Jewish relations. In the process, I met Professor Gad Yair, who introduced me for the first time to German social theory. In one of his classes we read "The Stranger," an essay by the German sociologist Georg Simmel. I connected deeply with the text. Simmel experienced his position as German-Jewish scholar as the perpetual outsider. As a German Jew he participated in German society but could never be fully German.

Almost twenty years later, I believe that "The Stranger" can provide important methodological insight for sociologists who are researching a population they are socioeconomically or culturally removed from. Simmel (1971) writes that "the stranger is . . . an element within the group that involves both being outside of it and confronting it" (144). Not being bound by deep, partisan ties to the community, the stranger, Simmel maintains, can be more objective than an insider. At the same time, he is familiar enough with the rules that govern social interactions to actively participate in the life of the group. Consequently, the stranger is not a detached observer but embodies "remoteness and nearness" simultaneously (145). As the outsider living within society, he brings qualities to the group that are not inherent to it (143).

I argue that it can be helpful for qualitative sociologists to become "strangers" in the Simmelian sense during fieldwork. Embracing the role of a stranger does not have to lead to exoticizing or vilifying marginalized communities, a practice Victor Rios famously termed the "jungle book trope" (2011). On the contrary, assuming the simultaneous nearness and distance of Simmel's stranger may allow us to reflect on our limitations in understanding the motivations, constraints, and cultural practices of the group we study. Being aware of one's position as a stranger in the field, I argue, encourages reflexivity and can prevent the kind of "Indiana Jones" or "cowboy" mentality that still prevails in some corners of qualitative sociology (Hanson and Richards 2019).

Of course, entering the field as a stranger does not presuppose the ability to capture the social world in its full complexity. "The stranger" ultimately remains excluded from the inner workings of the group. Assuming a liminal position between detachment and connection, however, has undeniable methodological advantages. Simmel points that out that a stranger is only a temporary group member. This transient social potion implies that he "often receives the most surprising revelations and confidences" (145). As Mario Luis Small (2017) argues in *Someone To Talk To*, people may feel more comfortable confiding in someone who represents a weak social tie. It is unlikely that a "stranger" could significantly harm one's reputation. Being a stranger in the field, therefore, can unearth data that may not be revealed to insiders.

During the data collection for this project, I assumed the role of a stranger in both field sites. Even though I am from Germany, I had not lived there for more than a decade and I was no longer up to date on contemporary German culture. Being a native to the area where I conducted my fieldwork still offered several advantages. For example, I understood the local dialect. I could also draw on old social networks dating back to high school to open doors. Since my professional life was now centered in the United States, I was nevertheless perceived as an outsider—the professor from New York rather than a researcher from southern Germany. Over the course of my fieldwork, I noticed how far removed I had become from my home country. Comparing the German prison to the American ones I had visited, the homogeneity of the prison staff struck me, especially in contrast to the majority of immigrant children they supervised. I also noticed how others applied racist labels that I myself had once used without thinking about them.

Being introduced to respondents as coming from New York, enabled me to position myself as the ideal-typical stranger. I looked and spoke like the people around me but my stake in the community was limited. My identity was not defined solely by the place I was from but by the city now I lived in. As a result, the respondents could open up about racism they had experienced growing up without threatening my identity as a southern German woman.

In hindsight, I was more at ease during fieldwork in the United States, where my status as a stranger was more obvious. My German accent immediately marks me as an outsider. At the same time, I am more attuned to the contemporary political and cultural debates that surfaced in my US interviews. My German background piqued the interest of the respondents in Pennsylvania, who had never met someone from Germany before. They were curious about what it was like where I grew up. They wanted to know why I came to the United States, and what I thought about American society. By the time I did fieldwork in Pennsylvania in 2014, I had several years of research in Boston and Chicago behind me. I had become familiar enough with the communities I studied to build rapport with the sorts of people living in them more easily.

During the data analysis, I attempted to reflect critically on the nuances I might have missed, and I focused on the differences between the two field sites that I was able to discern. Analyzing the German data, I attempted to take an "American perspective" on racism and inequality, while I sought to analyze the American data from a "German" viewpoint, applying ideas about social welfare, state intervention, and punishment that are taken for granted in Germany. I maintain that being a stranger in both places allowed me to notice different patterns of discrimination, and peculiarities about both punitive systems that I would have not been able to notice as an insider.

As I bring this project to a close, I contemplate the imperfections and limitations of sociological inquiry. Irrespective of our positionality, sociologists can never fully capture the social world in all its complexity. Our mere presence changes what we observe and can alter outcomes. Since qualitative sociologists can't measure their margin of error, finding our way back to a Weberian (1949) "objectivity" could be useful. Weber understood that our interests, be they personal or political, shape the topics we choose to investigate. Being aware of why we study what we study is key for acknowledging our own limitations in interpreting the data we collect. It is this kind of reflexive analysis that distinguishes sociological inquiry from journalism. Accepting uncertainty and inevitably incomplete representation, *The Price of Freedom* does not offer any easy solutions. All I can hope for is that a combination of the specific liminal positions I occupied in the field has raised some worthwhile questions.

AMERICAN AND GERMAN INTERVIEW GUIDES

AMERICAN INTERVIEW GUIDE
1. Life Course Interviews: Pine Grove
INTERVIEW 1) CURRENT SITUATION

<u>Demographics</u>
Name:
Date of Birth:
Last address before arrest:
Number of siblings:
Age of siblings:
Number of Children:

<u>Background Information</u>
Where were you born?
From the earliest time you remember, how many times did you move to a different place?
Can you recall the address that you lived from when you were born until your arrest? If you can, put the first address you remember, etc.
The respondent will be asked to fill out the following form:

Street Name	City, State	Year lived at address

What was the date of your arrest that led to you to come here?
How many times have you been arrested before?

Were you involved with the juvenile justice system?

Were you involved with the PA's child welfare system?

What other institutions other than Pine Grove have you been incarcerated in?

How long have you been in Pine Grove?

When will you be released?

Do you have any idea what you will be doing after you get out?

Daily Life in Pine Grove

Tell me about your daily routine here.

- What programs are you enrolled in?
- Can you describe a typical day for me?
- How often do you get visitors?
- What is the hardest thing about being incarcerated?

What is your main source of communication with people on the outside?

How often do you receive letters/phone calls/visits?

Who is the person you miss most? Why?

Neighborhood/Community

A map will be presented to the respondent that contains his final residential address, the school he attended/place of employment, as well as the place where he committed the crime that led to his arrest. (Information is based on the case files accessed before the first interview.) The respondent will be asked to mark on the map his movements immediately before his arrest.

Can you draw on this map the boundaries of what you would consider to be your neighborhood around the time of your arrest?

Can you tell me what a typical day looked like in the three months before you got arrested:

Where did you spend your days/nights during that time?

Can you retrace the way you typically took to get to school/work?

(Where did you get on the bus/subway?)

Can you show me on this map where you would typically hang out after school/work?

For example, if you wanted to play basketball or sports in general where would you go?

Was there a youth club you went to regularly? Where was it and how often did you go there?

Where would you go if you wanted to buy a beer? How often did you go to this store?

Were there any other stores that you went to frequently?

Can you show me where you would spend your time if you skipped school?

Who was usually with you during that time?

Can you show me on the map where you would meet your friends and which way you would take to get there?

How did your routine change on the weekends?

Where did you spend your days/nights?

What would you do on a typical Saturday or Sunday? Can you point out the places on the map where you would usually be on Saturdays or Sundays?

I would like you to think about the day you got arrested. What do you remember about that day?

- What was your original plan for that day?
- When you left the house, can you retrace the steps to your first destination that day?
- Where did you go after that? [Subway/bus stop]
- How did your plans change over the course of the day and why?
- Can you show me on this map the last stop you made before you got arrested?

[If inmate does not claim to be innocent] → What went through your mind right before you committed your crime?

If you look back on that day, what would you do differently?

Reflection on Crime/Arrest

Why do you think you ended up in Pine Grove?

- How old were you when you first got involved with the streets
- What was the first crime you committed?
  - o Do you remember why you did it?

- Who or what do you think is responsible for you being here?
- What could have changed your fate?

INTERVIEW 2) CHILDHOOD: AGE 0–12

The respondent will be shown a map/maps that indicate(s) the different addresses at which he has lived. Information about his residential history was gathered during the first interview.

Can you put a number on the different places that you lived at: 1 = first place I remember living, etc.

The respondent will additionally be asked to fill out the form below to verify his residential history and to fill in some of the missing information.

Residential History: Age 0–12

Address	Stayed there from XX until XX	People living in the same household	Main caretaker	Kindergarten attended elementary school (*if you attended several schools while you were living at a specific address, please list all of them*)

Which of these places did you stay longest? For how long did you live there?

Can you write down who lived with you at these different places?

Can you also write down who your main caretaker was when you were living there?

Did you attend preschool or kindergarten?

If yes, can you indicate where on the map your preschool and or kindergarten was?

Can you point out where you went to elementary school?

Which place did you like best/least? Why?

Family Life

Would you say your mother was an important part of your life then?

- Why? Why not?
- How often did you see her?

- Are you in touch with her now?
- Did it affect you that she was not a part of your life? How?/Why not?

Would you say father was an important part of your life?

- Why? Why not?
- How often did you see him?
- Are you in touch with him now?
- Did it affect you that he was not a part of your life? How?/Why not?

You mentioned that you have XX siblings Which one of your siblings were you particularly close to before you turned twelve and why?

- Are you still close to him/her now?

What is your first childhood memory?

What is the happiest memory that you have between the ages of three and twelve?/What were the happiest moments during this time?

If you look back on your childhood, was there anything that you think set you up for ending up at Pine Grove?

What is your most painful childhood memory?

Do you think you were a "problematic" child growing up?

- Why/Why not?

If you could change something about your childhood, what would that be?

Were any of your family members/household members involved in crime/gangs during your childhood?

Yes:

- How do you think that influenced you?

Were any family members/household members addicted to drugs/ alcohol while you were a child?

- How do you think that influenced you?

If respondent has children:

- What do you want to do different than your parents raising your child(ren)?

<u>Friends</u>

Respondent will again be shown the map that indicates the residential
history. The respondent will be asked to mark specific places that
were important during his childhood.

Who were your closest friends during that time?

Can you indicate on your map where your three closest friends lived
at the time? Please put initials after the place you indicated this.

How much time did you spent at their houses?

Can you describe what you and your friends would do when you hung
out together?

Can you indicate on the map the places you would spent your free
time at?

Prompt: Youth clubs, basketball court, playground.

- Are you still in touch with some of your childhood friends?

Where your friends at the time involved in crime/gangs?
Yes:

- How do you think that influenced you?

Who do you think had your friends at the time had more influence
on you at the time than your family/siblings or your friends?

<u>Educational Experience</u>

Did you attend preschool/kindergarten?

What do you remember about this time?

What do you remember about elementary school?

- Was there a teacher that you particularly liked?
- What did you not like about school? (teacher, classmates etc.)

<u>Social Services</u>

Did you work with a social worker/therapist, etc. before you turned
twelve?
Yes:

- What was your experience? (Helpful/not helpful, what did you get
  out of it?)

Did you take any medicine for example to deal with depression/ ADHD/mood swings during your childhood?

Yes:

- What did you take?
- Who prescribed them?
- Did it help you? Why?/How?/Why not?

<u>Role Models</u>

Was there anyone inside or outside of your family that you looked up to during childhood?

Yes:

- What did you admire about him/her?
- Are you still in touch with this person?
- How do you view him/her differently now?

No:

- Why was that the case?

INTERVIEW 3) ADOLESCENCE:

TWELVE UNTIL ARREST

The respondent will be shown a map/maps that indicate(s) the different addresses he has lived at between the ages of twelve until his arrest. Information about his residential history was gathered during the first interview.

The respondent will additionally be asked to fill out the form below to verify his residential history and to fill in some of the missing information.

Residential History: Aged twelve until arrest

Address	Stayed there from XX until XX	People living in the same household	Main caretaker	Middle school/ high school attended (*if you attended several schools while you were living at a specific address, please list all of them*)

Which of these places did you stay at longest? For how long did you live there?

Can you write down who lived with you at these different places?

Can you also write down who your main caretaker was when you were living there?

Which place you lived at did you like best/least? Why?

Can you describe how your life changed as you were growing up and turning into a teenager?

Can you share some of the happiest memories you have from that time?

If you could go back in time, what would you change about your teenage years and why would you change it?

<u>Family Life</u>

Would you say your mother was an important part of your life then?

- Why? Why not?
- How often did you see her?
- Are you in touch now?
- Did it affect you that she was not a part of your life? How?/Why not?

Would you say father was an important part of your life?

- Why? Why not?
- How often did you see him?
- Are you in touch now?
- Did it affect you that he was not a part of your life? How?/Why not?

You mentioned that you have XX siblings, which one of your siblings were you particularly close to after you turned twelve and why?

- Are you still close to him/her now?

What is the happiest memory that you have between the ages of twelve and your arrest?/What were the happiest moments during this time?

If you look back on your teenage years, was there anything that you think set you up for ending up at Pine Grove?

What is your most painful memory from that time?

Do you think you were a "problematic" teenager?

- Why/Why not?

If you could change something about your teenage years, what would that be?

If respondent has children:

- What do you want to do different than your parents raising your child(ren)?

Were any of your family members/household members involved in crime/gangs during your adolescence?

Yes:

- How do you think that influenced you?

Were any family members/household members addicted to drugs/alcohol while you were a teenager?

- How do you think that influenced you?

Which member of your family/household was most important to you at the time?

- Why?

Friends

Respondent will again be shown the map that indicates his residential history. The respondent will then be asked to mark specific places that were important meeting places for him and his friends during his adolescence.

Who were your closest friends during that time?

Can you indicate on your map where your three closest friends lived at the time? Please put initials after your mark.

How much time did you spent at their houses?

Can you describe what you and your friends would do when you hung out together?

Can you indicate on the map the places you would spent your free time at?

Prompt: Youth clubs, basketball court, playground.

- Are you still in touch with some of the friends you had during your teenage years?

Where your friends at the time involved in crime/gangs?
Yes:

- How do you think that influenced you?

Who do you think had your friends at the time had more influence on you at the time than your family/siblings or your friends?

Role Models

Was there anyone inside or outside of your family that you looked up to during childhood?
Yes:

- What did you admire about him/her?
- Are you still in touch with this person?
- How do you view him/her differently now?

No:

- Why was that the case?

Social Services

Were you involved with the juvenile justice system during that time?
Yes:

- Did you have a probation officer?

Yes:
- How many different probation officers did you have?
- How was your relationship with him/her?
- How often did you meet with him/her?
- Where would you meet with him/her?
- Was his office close to your home?

Yes: Take out map: Can you show me where the office was on this map. Please mark it and write after the mark how often during one typical week/month you would meet him/her.

- How would you typically get to his office/the place you would meet him/her? (Prompt what was the bus stop/subway station you used.)
- How did he/she help you/fail to help you?

Were you incarcerated?
Yes:

- Where and for how long?
- How did incarceration help you or failed to help you?
- What other programs were you enrolled in?
- Was there any social worker/probation officer/caseworker that you felt was supportive of you and wanted the best for you?

In your opinion was there anything that the juvenile justice system could have done to help you more effectively?

If you think back to the years before you committed the crime that led you here, what could you have done differently?

- Why did you not do this?
- How did you try to get away from the streets or other negative influences?

Were you involved with the Department of Children and Families?
Did you have a caseworker?
Yes:

- How was your relationship with him/her?
- How often did you meet with him/her?
- Where would you meet with him/her?
- Was his office close to your home?

Yes: Take out map: Can you show me where the office was on this map? Please mark it and write after the mark how often during one typical week/month you would meet him/her

- How would you typically get to his office/the place you would meet him/her? (Prompt what was the bus stop/subway station you used.)
- How did he/she help you/fail to help you?

Was there anything that you wish someone would have offered you that would have prevented you from ending up at Pine Grove?

<u>Educational Experience</u>
Respondent will be shown another map that covers the area he lived in as an adolescent.

Can you indicate where on the map your middle school(s) high school(s) was/were? Please indicate the year you attended this school after the mark you have made.

Can you map for me for each address you lived at, your way to and from school?

Can you mark the places that you would hang out after school?

If these places changed between twelve and the time of arrest please indicate the approximate time frame during which you regularly went to this place and how often during the week you would go there. For example: Youth club *X*; went there from ages twelve to fourteen every week.

Prompt: Basketball court, youth club, friend's houses.

What do you remember about your time in middle school/high school?

- Would you say you attended school regularly?
- Was there a teacher that you particularly liked?
- What did you not like about school? (teacher, classmates etc.)

<u>Future Plans</u>

Do you know where you are going to move to after you have been released?

How do you want to change your life once you are released? What do you want to do differently than before?

How do you think you can manage to stay out of trouble?

How do you think you can prepare for your life after your release while you are still in here?

2. Interviews with Outside Respondents

In addition to the questions below the interviews will be adjusted individually according to the information gathered from the case summary files and previous interviews with R.

<u>Demographics</u>

Name:

Date of Birth:

Relationship to R:

Racial background:

Occupation:

Highest level of education:

Relationship to Original Respondent

If not mother, father, sibling or other close relative.

When was the first time you met R?

How did you meet R?

- How would you describe your relationship to R?
- How close are you?
- Do you trust him? Why?/Why not?
- What do you think are his strength? What are his weaknesses?

Depending on when he/she met R:

- Can you tell me about his early childhood?
  - o What was he like as a toddler/child?
  - o How was he different from other children?
  - o Was he challenging child? Why?/Why not?
  - o What were his talents?
  - o Was there anything in his early childhood that you think could have contributed to him getting involved in crime?
- Can you tell me about his late childhood/teenage years?
  - o What was he like as a teenager?
  - o How was he different from other teenagers?
  - o Was he challenging as teenager? Why?/Why not?
  - o What were his talents?
  - o Was there anything in his late childhood/early teenage years that you think could have contributed to him getting involved in crime?
- What is your impression, what kind of support has R received from social service agencies over the years?
  - o Can you remember something specific that seemed helpful to him?
  - o Did he have a caseworker or probation officer that seemed helpful/supportive?
  - o Can you think of any type of intervention that could have helped him to stay away from the streets?

- As far as you know can you describe to me how R got involved in crime?
  - o Why do you think he ended up at Pine Grove?
  - o If R does not serve a life sentence: What is your prognosis, do you think R will get in trouble again after he is released?
  - o In your opinion, how could R be supported most effectively and what would it take to keep him out of prison after he is released?

Have you visited R in Pine Grove?

How do you stay in touch with him?

How regular is your contact with him?

What do you think does he get out of the program?

If you had to use one word to describe R what would that be?

GERMAN INTERVIEW GUIDE
In-Prison Interview

Können Sie den Tag beschreiben an dem Sie verhaftet worden sind?

Wieviele Male sind Sie zuvor verhaftet worden?

Waren Sie vor dieser Haftstrafe bereits am Jugendgericht?

Ja: Was war der Anlass?

Waren Sie jemals mit dem Jugendamt in Baden-Württemberg kontakt?

Ja: Wie sah dieser kontakt aus?

Sind Sie in anderen Institutionen inhaftiert gewesen?

Ja: Wie unterschiedet sich diese Institution von Adelmsheim?

Was werden Sie nach Ihrer Entlassung machen?

Wo werden Sie wohnen?

Mit wem werden Sie zusammen wohnen?

Haben Sie bereits Arbeit gefunden?

Ja: Wer war Ihnen bei der Arbeitsssuche behilflich?

Nein: Was sind Ihre Pläne? Wie werden Sie Arbeit finden? Wen werden Sie um Hilfe bitten?

Wird Sie jemand am Tag Ihrer Entlassung abholen?

Was wird das Erste sein dass Sie nach Ihrer Entlassung tun werden?

Was werden Sie tun um nicht mit dem Gesetz in Konflikt zu geraten?

Gibt es Leute die Sie vermeiden werden nach Ihrer Entlassung?

Was haben Sie in Ihrer Zeit in Adelsheim gelernt?

Wer war Ihnen am meisten behilflich während ihrer Zeit in Adelsheim?

- Wer stand Ihnen bei?
- Von wem sind Sie enttäuscht?
- Welcher Beamte in der JVA war besonders hilfsbereit und hat Sie unterstützt?

Wie stellen Sie sich ihr Leben in einem Jahr im Idealfall vor?

Was denken Sie wird am schwierigsten für Sie sein nach Ihrer Entlassung?

Denken Sie dass Sie Leute kontaktieren werden mit denen Sie keinen Kontakt hatten in Adelsheim?

Ja: Wen?

Alltag in Adelsheim

Erzählen Sie mir wie der Tagesablauf hier aussieht.

Was ist das schwierigste daran eingesperrt zu sein?

Wen vermissen Sie am meisten und warum?

Ich würde Sie gerne nach Ihrer Entlassung noch einmal kontaktieren.

Hätten Sie Interesse an einem weiteren Interview?

Ja

Nein

Ja: Können Sie mir eine Addresse/Telefonnummer geben unter der ich sie draussen erreichen könnte?

Outside Interviews

<u>Daily Life after Release</u>

Erzählen Sie mir bitte wie Ihr Leben nach der Entlassung:

Wo wohnen Sie?

Sind Sie mit ihrer momentanen Wohnsituation zufrieden?

Bei wem wohnen Sie?

Haben Sie eine Arbeitsstelle gefunden?

Nein: Warum denken Sie dass Ihre Arbeitssuche bisher erfolglos verlaufen ist?

Ja: Was für eine Arbeitsstelle haben Sie gefunden? Sind Sie zufrieden mit der Arbeitsstelle? Warum/Warum nicht? Wer hat Ihnen bei der Arbeitssuche geholfen? Wer sind Ihre Arbeitskollegen?

Beschreiben Sie bitte Ihren Alltag:
Wann stehen Sie auf?
Was machen Sie dann?
Wann gehen Sie zu Bett?

An welchen Wiedereingliederungsmassnahmen haben Sie teilgenommen?
Welche Massnahmen waren hilfreich? Warum? Warum nicht?
Wie oft stehen Sie mit Ihrem Bewährungshelfer in Kontakt?
Erhalten Sie therapeutische Unterstuetzung?

<u>Current Impact of Incarceration</u>
Gibt es jemanden aus der JVA den Sie vermissen/mit dem Sie gerne
    sprechen würden?
Warum? Warum nicht?
Wer wäre das?
Was glauben Sie inwiefern hat der Aufenthalt in JVA Adelsheim den
    Umgang mit Ihren Freunden verändert?
Inwiefern beeinflusst das Gefängnis noch heute Ihre psychologische
    Verfassung?
Träume?
Haben Sie angst davor ins Gefängnis zurück zu müssen? Warum?/
    Warum nicht?

Was hat sich in ihrer Nachbarschaft, bei Freunden und der Familie
    verändert als Sie im Gefängnis waren?
Sind Sie seit Ihrer Entlassung in Versuchung geraten eine Straftat zu
    begehen?
Warum?/Warum nicht?

<u>Emotions</u>
Was war der glücklichste Moment für Sie seit der Entlassung?
Gibt es etwas dass Sie traurig gemacht hat seit Sie entlassen worden sind?
Gab es etwas dass Sie wütend gemacht hat?
Warum?/Warum nicht?
Ihrer Einschätzung nach, gehen Sie mit Ihren Emotionen jetzt anders
    um als vor Ihrer Gefängnissstrafe?

Wenn Sie etwas an ihrem Leben im Augenblick verändern könnten, was wäre das?

Social Ties
Welche Person steht Ihnen im Augenblick am Nächsten?
Warum?
Wieviel Zeit verbringen Sie mit Ihr/Ihm?
Mit wem verbringen Sie sonst noch Zeit?
Verbringen Sie Zeit mit andern als Gruppe?
Wer hat bisher einen guten Einfluss auf Sie ausgeübt?
Warum?
Gibt es Leute die Sie vermeiden? Warum?

Future Outlook
Wie wird es Ihnen gelingen auf Dauer nicht Rückfällig zu werden?
Wie schwer glauben Sie wird es eine Arbeitsstelle zu finden?

- Haben Sie bereits eine Stelle in Aussicht?
- Wie wird es Ihnen gelingen auf Dauer nüchtern zu bleiben, keine Drogen mehr zu nehmen?
- Wie schwer wird es Ihnen fallen mit weniger Geld als zuvor auszukommen?
- Was glauben Sie wieviel Geld werden Sie benötigen?

Was möchten Sie innerhalb der nächsten sechs Monate erreichen?
Für wie wahrscheinlich halten Sie es dass Sie wieder in die Kriminalität abrutschen?
Warum?
Gibt es irgendetwas dass Sie gerne hinzufügen wuerden?
Vielen Dank für Ihre Teilnahme.

NOTES

INTRODUCTION: A NEW PHASE
FOR CRIMINAL JUSTICE REFORM

1. Messner and Rosenfeld's *Crime and the American Dream*, originally published more than two decades ago, is a notable exception. I have used the following edition: Steven F. Messner and Richard Rosenfeld, *Crime and the American Dream* (Belmont, CA: Wadsworth, 2007).

2. Nicholas Turner and Jeremy Travis, "What We Learned from German Prisons," *New York Times*, August 6, 2015, https://www.nytimes.com/2015/08/07/opinion/what-we-learned-from-german-prisons.html.

3. ACLU Press Release, "91 Percent of Americans Support Criminal Justice Reform, ACLU Polling Finds," ACLU.org, November 16, 2017, https://www.aclu.org/press-releases/91-percent-americans-support-criminal-justice-reform-aclu-polling-finds.

4. "Executive Order on Reforming Our Incarceration System," White House, January 26, 2021, https://www.whitehouse.gov/briefing-room/presidential-actions/2021/01/26/executive-order-reforming-our-incarceration-system-to-eliminate-the-use-of-privately-operated-criminal-detention-facilities/. In 1989, Senator Biden demanded action from the Bush administration: "We need another D-Day. Instead, you're giving us another Vietnam: a limited war, fought on the cheap, financed on the sly, with no clear objectives, and ultimately destined

for stalemate and human tragedy." See David Farber, "The War on Drugs Turns 50 Today," *Washington Post*, June 17, 2021, https://www.washingtonpost.com/outlook/2021/06/17/war-drugs-turns-50-today-its-time-make-peace/.

5. See Elizabeth A. Harris, "Inside Kim Kardashian's Prison-Reform Machine," *New York Times*, April 2, 2020, https://www.nytimes.com/2020/04/02/arts/television/kim-kardashian-prison-reform.html.

6. In recent poll conducted by the Pew Research Center, 85 percent of American respondents and 71 percent of German respondents described the bilateral relationship between both countries as good. See "U.S.-German Relations on the Mend as New Leadership Takes Hold," Pew Research Center, November 22, 2021, https://www.pewresearch.org/global/2021/11/22/u-s-german-relations-on-the-mend-as-new-leadership-takes-hold/; The Berlin Pulse, accessed April 28, 2023, https://www.koerber-stiftung.de/en/the-berlin-pulse.

7. Because of IRB stipulation and limited resources I had to exclude those incarcerated young people who are under eighteen. I would have needed to get parental consent to secure the children's participation in the study and it would delayed approval of the study.

8. In addition to its Young Adult Offender Program, SCI Pine Grove also houses adults serving time as part of the general population. As of May 2016, 926 people were incarcerated there. Approximately three hundred young men were usually part of the Young Adult Offender Program. This information is based on a conference call with the superintendent of Pine Grove on March 27, 2014 (Department of Corrections 2016).

9. See *Pennsylvania Juvenile Act (2008)*, accessed April 28, 2023, https://www.ova.pa.gov/AboutOVA/CrimeVictimsRights/Documents/Juvenile_Act_2008.pdf.

10. One participant was sent to the restricted housing unit after I conducted the first interview and could not be reinterviewed over the course of the study.

11. Those older than twenty-one may have had their juvenile probation revoked but could still serve their juvenile sentence at JVA Adelsheim despite their advanced age.

12. Having a "migration background" indicates that one or both of the youths' parents are not ethnically German.

13. "Kriminologischer Dienst" is part of the research branch of the ministry of justice in Baden-Württemberg. This particular research group is located at the prison in Adelsheim and focuses on young people held at this institution.

14. For reporting about abuse in the Pennsylvania Juvenile Justice System that some respondents disclosed in interviews, see Lisa Gartner, "On Their Own: How Pennsylvania Failed to Protect Boys from Abuse at Glen Mills and Other State-Licensed Juvenile Programs," *Philadelphia Inquirer*, October 3, 2019, https://www.inquirer.com/news/a/pennsylvania-reform-school-abuse-scandal-dhs-oversight-glen-mills-20191003.html.

15. Pennsylvania State Police, *Firearms Annual Report, 2020*, accessed March 5, 2022, https://www.psp.pa.gov/firearms-information/Firearms%20Annual%20report/Pennsylvania_State_Police_2020_Firearms_Annual_Report.pdf.

16. Florian Durr, "Zahl der Waffen im Südwesten steigt an," Stuttgarter Nachrichten, January 18, 2022, https://www.stuttgarter-nachrichten.de/inhalt.sicherheit-in-baden-wuerttemberg-zahl-der-waffen-im-suedwesten-steigt-an.ff6227f9-bc79-4b93-a32e-f7d86793649f.html; "Baden-Württemberg in Zahlen: Bevölkerung," Baden-Württemberg.de, accessed April 28, 2023, https://www.baden-wuerttemberg.de/de/unser-land/land-und-leute/bevoelkerung/.

17. "Homicide Mortality by State," CDC, 2020, accessed October 12, 2022, https://www.cdc.gov/nchs/pressroom/sosmap/homicide_mortality/homicide.htm; Ministerium für inneres, Digitalisierung und Migration, *Sicherheit 2020: Sicherheitsbericht des Landes Baden-Württemberg*, accessed April 28, 2023, https://im.baden-wuerttemberg.de/fileadmin/redaktion/m-im/intern/dateien/publikationen/20210219_Sicherheitsbericht_Baden_Wuerttemberg_2020.pdf.

18. "Straftaten und Verurteilte: Erfasste Straftaten, Tatverdächtige und Aufklärungsquoten," Baden Württemberg: Staatisches Landesamt, accessed April 28, 2023, https://www.statistik-bw.de/Rechtspflege/StraftatenVerurt/LRt0401.jsp?TSPD_101_R0=083bd47448ab20004ed5ff490f64239a60629671f2feda8953b7bddb93b2a0ef82fc9815eeae251e0

8368cd4d5143000af308ff4c90fb61752588a282ecef7ecff7ffif2a0b0d04f950
8739eb9ab00a9695d8c11b4d3d53ea64ef4624ae05184.

19. One challenge of comparing the rates of violent crime in both areas involves the different conventions of classifying criminals in both countries—for example, defining an act as a murder as opposed to manslaughter. In Germany, the burden for sentencing someone for murder is much higher for the prosecution than in the United States. See § 211 StGB, accessed April 28, 2023, https://www.gesetze-im-internet.de/stgb/__211.html. In order to sentence someone to life in prison for murder, it must be demonstrated that the act has been committed based on "low motives" (niedrige Beweggründe)—for example, greed or the desire to witness another person's death (Mordlust). In practice this means that killings committed under the influence of alcohol or drugs may not be considered murder when the victim is not known to the perpetrator and the prepetrator's ability to make decisions was compromised. Consequently, cases that might be classified as manslaughter in Germany would likely be tried as a murder case in the United States. For the German definition of manslaughter, see § 212, StGB, accessed April 28, 2023, https://www.gesetze-im-internet.de/stgb/__212.html.

20. Cf. Nicholas Turner and Jeremy Travis, "What We Learned from German Prisons," *New York Times*, August 6, 2015, https://www.nytimes.com/2015/08/07/opinion/what-we-learned-from-german-prisons.html.

CHAPTER ONE. HOMOGENEITY, PUNISHMENT,
AND THE WELFARE STATE

1. See, for example, the recall of San Francisco District Attorney Chesa Boudin in June 2022: "Voters in San Francisco Topple the City's Progressive District Attorney, Chesa Boudin," *New York Times*, June 8, 2022, https://www.nytimes.com/2022/06/07/us/politics/chesa-boudin-recall-san-francisco.html.

2. "Keine Nachsicht für Feinde unserer Ordnung," *Der Spiegel*, July 25, 1976, https://www.spiegel.de/politik/keine-nachsicht-fuer-feinde-unserer-ordnung-a-bf4b47f8-0002-0001-0000-000041157595.

3. "Unrechtjustiz," Gedenkstätte Plötzensee, accessed April 28, 2023, https://www.gedenkstaette-ploetzensee.de/unrechtsjustiz.

4. See article 102 of the German constitution: Grundgesetz für die Bundesrepublik Deutschland Art. 102, Bundesministerium der Justiz: Bundesamt für Justiz, accessed April 28, 2023, https://www.gesetze-im-internet.de/gg/art_102.html.

5. See article 102 GG: Die Todesstrafe ist abgeschafft [The death penalty is abolished], Bundesministerium der Justiz: Bundesamt für Justiz, accessed April 28, 2023, https://www.gesetze-im-internet.de/gg/art_102.html.

6. Michael Schlieben, "Was, wenn das hier im Grundgesetz gelandet wäre?" *Zeit Online*, May 23, 2019, https://www.zeit.de/wissen/2019-05/deutschland-70-30-grundgesetz-alternativen-gleichberechtigung/komplettansicht.

7. As Evans reconstructs in *Rituals of Retribution* (1997), one of the strongest advocates against the death penalty was the nationalist party DP (Deutsche Partei). In a strange alliance with the SPD (Social Democratic Party), Evans argued, the DP was primarily interested in protecting its constituency—namely, former Wehrmacht soldiers and nationalist refugees from East Prussia.

8. Auschwitz Committee is a postwar international organization based in Vienna representing Auschwitz survivors.

9. See Werner Renz, "Der Frankfurter Auschwitz Prozess," Tonbandmitschnitte des Auschwitz-Prozesses (1963–1965), accessed April 28, 2023, https://www.auschwitz-prozess.de/materialien/T_02_Der_Frankfurter_Auschwitz-Prozess/.

10. The case of Adolf Rögner—that is, his contributions to the Auschwitz trials and other investigations—is complex and cannot be fully accounted for here. His role in, as well as the impact other "career criminals" had on, bringing former Nazis to justice is the subject of my current research and will be discussed in future publications.

11. *New York Times*, January 17, 1964; *New York Times*, 7, May 16, 1964, 2.

12. See the documents in the Federal Archive of Germany, BArch, B 162/ 2734; and the State Archive of Baden-Württemberg LABW StAL, EL 333 III B 88.

13. The statute of limitations for persecution of manslaughter, for example, was ten years at the time. Since German courts regained jurisdiction in 1950, manslaughter committed during the Nazi regime could no longer be persecuted after 1960. See Robert A Monson, "The

West German Statute of Limitations on Murder: A Political, Legal, and Historical Exposition," *American Journal of Comparative Law* 30, no. 4 (1982): 605–25.

14. While individual responsibility for specific terror attacks remains unsolved, RAF members collectively faced unusually long prison sentences. See "Was aus den RAF-Mitgliedern wurde (Auswahl)," *Süddeutsche Zeitung*, January 19, 2016, https://www.sueddeutsche.de/politik/raf-die-drei-generationen-der-roten-armee-fraktion-1.893822-2.

15. See, for example, Peter Burghardt, Annette Ramelsberger, Antonie Rietzschel, and Ronen Steink, "Auf dem rechten Auge blind? Nach einem brutalen Überfall in Ballstädt kommen neun Neonazis mit Bewährung davon—solche milden Urteile gibt es zuhauf an deutschen Gerichten: Zwölf Fälle," *Süddeutsche Zeitung*, July 16, 2021, https://www.sueddeutsche.de/projekte/artikel/politik/die-deutsche-justiz-auf-dem-rechten-auge-blind-e719583/?reduced=true.

16. See paragraph 129a StGB, Bundesministerium der Justiz: Bundesamt für Justiz, accessed April 28, 2023, https://www.gesetze-im-internet.de/stgb/__129a.html.

17. "Darlehensrückzahlung," Bundesministerium für Bildung und Forschung, August 1, 2022, https://www.bafög.de/bafoeg/de/antrag-stellen/merkblaetter/darlehensrueckzahlung/darlehensrueckzahlung_node.html.

18. "What Can SNAP Buy?" USDA Food and Nutrition Service, April 14, 2021, https://www.fns.usda.gov/snap/eligible-food-items.

19. "Housing Choice Vouchers Fact Sheet," US Department of Housing and Urban Development, accessed April 28, 2023, https://www.hud.gov/topics/housing_choice_voucher_program_section_8.

20. Ronald Reagan popularized the image of Black women living a lavish lifestyle on the public's dime, declaring during his primary campaign in New Hampshire: "There is a woman in Chicago, they found a woman who holds the record. She used 80 names, 30 addresses, 15 telephone numbers to collect food stamps, Social Security, veterans' benefits for four nonexistent, deceased veteran husbands, as well as welfare. Her tax-free cash income alone has been running $150,000 a year." See "'Welfare Queen' Becomes Issue in Reagan Campaign," *New York Times*, February 15, 1976, 51.

21. See Uwe Jahn, "Was sich mit dem Bürgergeld ändert," January 1, 2023, https://www.tagesschau.de/inland/innenpolitik/buergergeld-start-101.html.

22. "Quick Facts," US Census Bureau, accessed April 28, 2023, https://www.census.gov/quickfacts/fact/table/US/PST045221#qf-headnote-a.

23. "Bevölkerung: Migration und Integration," Destatis: Statistisches Bundesamt, accessed April 28, 2023, https://www.destatis.de/DE/Themen/Gesellschaft-Umwelt/Bevoelkerung/Migration-Integration/_inhalt.html.

24. See, for example, Jessica Benko, "The Radical Humaneness of Norway's Halden Prison: The Goal of the Norwegian Penal System Is to Get Inmates out of It," *New York Times*, March 29, 2015, https://www.nytimes.com/2015/03/29/magazine/the-radical-humaneness-of-norways-halden-prison.html; Natalie Moore, "No Bars, No Chains, No Locks: How Finland Is Reimagining Incarceration: A Third of Finnish Prisons Operate as 'Open,' Allowing Inmates to Leave the Facility for Work or School," WBEZ, November 15, 2021, https://www.wbez.org/stories/how-finlands-criminal-justice-system-compares-to-the-us/288505cf-365b-4508-a850-5106f551ce3e.

25. A recent case in point concerns the BioNTech founders Uğur Şahin and Özlem Türeci, whose "migration background" has been extensively marveled over by the German press. See Steffen Klusmann, "Ein deutsches Heldenpaar," *Der Spiegel*, December 31, 2020, 6.

CHAPTER TWO. THE UNCERTAINTY
OF BELONGING: NARRATIVES OF DIFFERENCE
AND EXCLUSION IN GERMANY
AND THE UNITED STATES

1. Notable exceptions are Loïc Wacquant's *Urban Outcasts: A Comparative Sociology of Advanced Marginality* (Cambridge: Polity Press, 2006), Lynn Haney's *Inventing the Needy: Gender and Politics of Welfare in Hungary* (Berkeley: University of California Press, 2002), and Michèle Lamont's *The Dignity of Working Men: Morality and the Boundaries of Race, Class, and Immigration* (Cambridge, MA: Harvard University Press, 2000).

2. "Quick Facts," US Census Bureau, accessed April 28, 2023, https://www.census.gov/quickfacts/fact/table/US/RHI725219.

3. The heading "We shovel a grave in the air" is from Paul Celan's poem "Todesfuge" ("Death Fugue") (1948).

4. After the official dissolution of the Holy Roman Empire in 1806 and until the founding of the second German Reich in 1871, Baden-Württemberg, the state where I conducted interviews, was its own kingdom, as were Prussia and Bavaria.

5. See, for example, the Romantic German Jewish poet Heinrich Heine, who wrote "Die Lorelei," a poem that to this day embodies German "Kultur."

6. In 1951, article 131 of the German Grundgesetz (basic law) officially paved the way for reinstating civil servants who had occupied roles in now defunct ministries or administrative branches before 1945 (see Perels 2004).

7. "Bevölkerung: Migration und Integration," Destatis: Statistisches Bundesamt, accessed April 28, 2023, https://www.destatis.de/DE/Themen/Gesellschaft-Umwelt/Bevoelkerung/Migration-Integration/_inhalt.html.

8. The transcript shows that after his omission I start to laugh and finish his sentence, saying "not just a little . . ." Picking up on his omission, I am not saying the word *Nazi* either. Contextually, it is obvious that he tries to avoid referring to ethnic Germans as Nazis since I am ethnically German. The impact of my own identity on these interviews will be discussed in greater depth in the appendix.

9. Echoing the extremely negative view of Roma in Germany, he referred to them with the derogatory term *Zigeuner* (gypsy).

10. The word does not have the same loaded significance in German but it is still considered inappropriate.

11. "Quick Facts," US Census Bureau, https://www.census.gov/quick facts/fact/table/US/RHI725219.

CHAPTER THREE. "HERE, I GET THREE MEALS
A DAY": SEGREGATION AND THE
RELATIVE EXPERIENCE OF POVERTY

1. See Amy O'Leary, "What Is Middle Class in Manhattan?," *New York Times,* January 18, 2013, https://www.nytimes.com/2013/01/20/realestate/what-is-middle-class-in-manhattan.html.

2. Some of the interview excerpts have appeared in prior publications. They are reused here to emphasize the comparative perspective.

3. "Undergraduate Cost of Attendance," University of Pennsylvania, Student Registration and Financial Services, accessed April 28, 2023, https://srfs.upenn.edu/costs-budgeting/undergraduate-cost-attendance.

4. See the publicly available data from the project at "Economic Diversity and Student Outcomes at the University of Pennsylvania," *New York Times*, accessed April 28, 2023, https://www.nytimes.com/interactive/projects/college-mobility/university-of-pennsylvania.

5. "About," University of Pennsylvania, Office of Investments, accessed April 28, 2023, https://investments.upenn.edu/about-us.

6. Oona Goodin-Smith, Ellie Rushing, and Anna Orso, "City Workers Clear Two Encampments on Kensington Avenue," *Philadelphia Inquirer*, August 18, 2021, https://www.inquirer.com/news/philadelphia-clears-evicts-homeless-encampments-kensington-20210818.html.

7. For more information about this opportunity, see, "Mutter-Kind-Kur und Vater-Kind-Kur," AOK, accessed April 28, 2023, https://www.aok.de/pk/leistungen/kuren-reha/mutter-kind-kur-und-vater-kind-kur/.

8. Economic statistics confirm this part of Germany is among the wealthiest in the entire country. In 2018, only Bavaria had a GDP that was higher than Baden-Wuerttemberg's 511,420 million euros. See "Arbeitskreis Volkswirtschaftliche Gesamtrechnungen der Länder," Statistische Ämter des Bundes und der Länder, accessed April 28, 2023, https://www.statistikportal.de/de/vgrdl/ergebnisse-laenderebene/bruttoinlandsprodukt-bruttowertschoepfung/bip#9517.

9. See "Kabinett beschließt Nachtragshaushalt," *Stuttgarter Zeitung*, October 23, 2018, https://www.stuttgarter-zeitung.de/inhalt.kabinett-beschliesst-nachtragshaushalt-spendabel.fac26e91-9811-4388-a563-cf7c3fa99d19.html.

10. See "Estimated Accidental and Undetermined Drug Overdose Deaths 2012–Current," Open Data PA, accessed April 28, 2023, https://data.pa.gov/Opioid-Related/Estimated-Accidental-and-Undetermined-Drug-Overdos/m3mg-va8e.

11. An example of such a limited government welfare program is the Low-Income Home Energy Assistance Program, which helps families to pay for their energy costs (Department of Human Services 2018a).

12. According to data recently published by the German ministry of labor and social work, about 37,500 people live unsheltered on German streets. Eighty percent of these are single men. In 2019, the United States counted roughly 103,000 people living unsheltered across the different states. More relevant is the number of people who are homeless but are not necessarily forced to live on the streets. In a single night in 2020, about 580,000 people were homeless in the United States out of a population of about 330 million. Over the course of seven nights in 2022, the German government counted around 86,700 as homeless people out of a population of roughly 86 million people. See *Forschungsbericht 605*, Bundesministerium für Arbeit und Soziales, September 2022, https://www.bmas.de/SharedDocs/Down loads/DE/Publikationen/Forschungsberichte/fb-605-empirische-unter suchung-zum-wohnungslosenberichterstattungsgesetz.pdf;jsessionid =843AC9AD6B2C92D5897ABA36E691807F.delivery1-replication?__blob =publicationFile&v=1; "Tools for Action," US Interagency Council on Homelessness, accessed April 28, 2023, https://www.usich.gov/tools-for -action/map/#fn[]=100&fn[]=200&fn[]=0&fn[]=0&fn[]=0&usheltered =true&year=2019.

CHAPTER FOUR. RETRIBUTION AND
DOMINATION: LIVING THROUGH PUNISHMENT
IN GERMANY AND THE UNITED STATES

1. *30 Jahre Justizvollzugsanstalt Heimsheim: 1990–2020*, June 24, 2020, https://km-bw.de/pb/site/jum2/get/documents/jum1/JuM/Justizvol lzugsanstalt%20Heimsheim/2020.06.24%20%20-%20Medieninforma tion%2030%20Jahre%20JVA%20Heimsheim.pdf.

2. Cf. Nicholas Turner and Jeremy Travis, "What We Learned from German Prisons," *New York Times*, August 6, 2015, https://www.ny times.com/2015/08/07/opinion/what-we-learned-from-german-prisons .html.

3. Vera Institute of Justice, "What German Prisons Do Differently," August 23, 2018, YouTube video, 3:15, https://www.youtube.com/watch?v =5uAIf_-rdMA.

4. "Die Nordreportage," programm.ARD.de, November 12, 2012, https://programm.ard.de/TV/ndrfsnds/die-nordreportage/eid_282269027843730.

5. "Hamburg-Fuhlsbüttel," KZ-Gedenkstätte Neuengamme, accessed April 28, 2023, https://www.kz-gedenkstaette-neuengamme.de/en/history/satellite-camps/satellite-camps/hamburg-fuhlsbuettel/.

6. Michaela Soyer, "Die Einsamkeit des Karl H." taz Archiv, accessed April 28, 2023, https://taz.de/Archiv-Suche/!1161066&s=Michaela%2BSoyer&SuchRahmen=Print/.

7. Under the purview of this law Roland Freisler's widow was able to secure her husband's pension, and she received generous government support until her death in 1997. Freisler, who died in 1945 during an air raid in Berlin, had been the leading judge of the special court between 1942 and 1945. In this capacity he was responsible for many death sentences of prominent members of the resistance. Among those he sentenced to death were Hans and Sophie Scholl of the resistance group, the White Rose. See *Der Spiegel*, February 2, 1985, https://www.spiegel.de/politik/kleines-zubrot-a-f8948a72-0002-0001-0000-000013512519.

8. Close to three million (2.7) German soldiers died on the Eastern Front (Hartmann 2003).

9. See StGB § 66, accessed April 28, 2023, https://www.gesetze-im-internet.de/stgb/__66.html.

10. Alexandra Kölle, "Bevölkerung mit Migrationshintergrund in Baden-Württemberg," Baden-Württemberg Statistisches Landesamt, *Inhaltsübersicht Monatsheft*, April 2017, https://www.statistik-bw.de/Service/Veroeff/Monatshefte/20170403; "Bevölkerung seit 2011 nach Nationalität, Altersjahren und Geschlecht," Baden-Württemberg Statistisches Landesamt, accessed April 28, 2023, https://www.statistik-bw.de/BevoelkGebiet/MigrNation/010352xx.tab?R=LA.

11. See "Briefverkehr," Justizvollzugsanstalt Adelsheim, accessed April 28, 2023, https://jva-adelsheim.justiz-bw.de/pb/,Lde/Startseite/Service/Briefe.

12. For a more comprehensive review of these issues, see chapter 3.

13. For the legal basis of German welfare services directed at children and families, see *Kinder- und Jugendhilfe: Achtes Buch Sozialgesetzbuch*, Bundesministerium für Familie, Senioren, Frauen und

Jugend, accessed April 28, 2023, https://www.bmfsfj.de/resource/blob/94106/40b8c4734ba05dad4639ca34908ca367/kinder-und-jugendhilfegesetz-sgb-viii-data.pdf.

14. The case files did not mention any specific illness his mother had; but, based on the symptoms Carl described, she likely suffered from pancreatitis.

15. See VAW (2019).

16. The average sentence length at Adelsheim in 2019 was twenty months (Stelly and Thomas 2021).

17. Karin Laub, "AfD Chief: Nazi Era a 'Speck of Bird Poop' in German History," Associated Press, June 2, 2018, https://apnews.com/article/social-media-ap-top-news-middle-east-germany-international-news-35a927e3ae954fa386a9e2406ae4439a.

18. "Distribution of Seats in the 20th German Bundestag," Deutscher Bundestag, accessed April 28, 2023, https://www.bundestag.de/en/parliament/plenary/distributionofseats.

CHAPTER FIVE. "I WANNA BE SOMEBODY":
EDUCATION AND UPWARD MOBILITY
IN GERMANY AND THE UNITED STATES

1. Schooling in Germany is regulated at the state level, and regulations differ from state to state. While in southern states the classic division between different types of school takes place after fourth grade, Berlin, for example, begins to separate students after sixth grade. This chapter focuses on schooling in Baden-Württemberg.

2. In 2012, the government of Baden-Württemberg introduced the concept of "community schools" (*Gemeinschaftsschulen*), where student of all levels are taught together until tenth grade. Lower-achieving students increasingly chose this type of school at the cost of traditional vocational schools, whose enrollment plummeted from 36 percent in 1990 to 6 percent during the 2019–20 school year. See also "Hauptschule—Restschule?" Deutschlandfunk, November 15, 2002, https://www.deutschlandfunk.de/hauptschule-restschule-100.html.

3. In 2015–16, the average at intake was 19.5 years.

4. See also *Berufsbildungsbericht* 2017, Bundesministerium für Bildung und Forschung, accessed April 28, 2023, https://www.bmbf.de/

SharedDocs/Publikationen/de/bmbf/3/31295_Berufsbildungsbericht_2017.pdf?__blob=publicationFile&v=3.

5. Jennifer Percy, "Trapped by the 'Walmart of Heroin,'" *New York Times Magazine*, October 10, 2018, https://www.nytimes.com/2018/10/10/magazine/kensington-heroin-opioid-philadelphia.html.

6. The exact location and name of the school are not disclosed in order to protect Jesus's identity.

7. For recent developments, see "Kopftuch in der Schule? Neuer Streit um Neutralitätsgesetz," *Zeit Online*, February 9, 2021, https://www.zeit.de/news/2021-02/09/scheeres-legt-beschwerde-gegen-kopftuch-urteil-ein?utm_referrer=https%3A%2F%2Fwww.google.com%2F; "Kopftuchverbot verstößt gegen Grundgesetz," video, *Frankfurter Allgemeine Zeitung*, accessed April 28, 2023, https://www.faz.net/aktuell/politik/bundesverfassungsgericht-kippt-kopftuchverbot-an-deutschen-schulen-13482702.html; Andrea Dernbach, "Vom Tattoo- zum Kopftuchverbot? Gesetzentwurf 'beunruhigt muslimische Lehrerinnen und Schulen,'" May 11, 2021, https://www.tagesspiegel.de/politik/vom-tattoo-zum-kopftuchverbot-gesetzentwurf-beunruhigt-muslimische-lehrerinnen-und-schulen/27177026.html.

8. For the law regulating religious instruction, see "Religionslehre ev: Evangelischer Religionsunterricht in Baden-Württemberg," Regierungspräsidien Baden-Württemberg, accessed April 28, 2023, https://rp.baden-wuerttemberg.de/themen/bildung/lehrer/unterricht/faecher/seiten/religionslehre-ev/.

9. See also *Berufsbildungsbericht* 2017, Bundesministerium für Bildung und Forschung, accessed April 28, 2023, https://www.bmbf.de/SharedDocs/Publikationen/de/bmbf/3/31295_Berufsbildungsbericht_2017.pdf?__blob=publicationFile&v=3.

10. Emily Rueb, "Schools Find a New Way to Combat Student Absences: Washing Machines," *New York Times*, March 13, 2019, https://www.nytimes.com/2019/03/13/us/schools-laundry-rooms.html.

WORKS CITED

Adorno, Theodor W. 1950. *Studien zum zum autoritären Charakter.* Frankfurt: Suhrkamp.

———. 2019. *Aspekte des neuen Rechtsradikalismus.* Frankfurt: Suhrkamp.

Aizer, Anna, Shari Eli, Joseph Ferrie, and Adriana Lleras-Muney. 2016. "The Long-Run Impact of Cash Transfers to Poor Families." *American Economic Review* 106, no. 4: 935–71.

Alba, Richard D., John R. Logan, and Kyle Crowder. 1997. "White Ethnic Neighborhoods and Assimilation: The Greater New York Region, 1980–1990." *Social Forces* 75, no. 3: 883–912.

Alba, Richard D., Amy Lutz, and Elena Vesselinov. 2001. "How Enduring Were the Inequalities among European Immigrant Groups in the United States?" *Demography* 38, no. 3: 349–56.

Alexander, Michelle. 2010. *The New Jim Crow.* New York: New Press.

Anderson, Benedict. 1991. *Imagined Communities.* London: Verso.

Anderson, Elijah. 1999. *Code of the Street: Decency, Violence, and the Moral Life of the Inner City.* New York: W. W. Norton.

Anil, Merih. 2007. "Explaining the Naturalisation Practices of Turks in Germany in the Wake of the Citizenship Reform of 1999." *Journal of Ethnic and Migration Studies* 33, no. 8: 1363–76.

Anyon, Y., C. Lechuga, D. Ortega, B. Downing, E. Greer, and J. Simmons. 2018. "An Exploration of the Relationships between Student Racial

Background and the School Sub-contexts of Office Discipline Referrals: A Critical Race Theory Analysis." *Race Ethnicity and Education* 21:390–406. https://doi.org/10.1080/13613324.2017.1328594.

Arendt, Hannah. 1944. "Race-Thinking before Racism." *Review of Politics* 6, no. 1: 36–73.

Aust, Stefan. 2008. *Der Baader Meinhof Komplex.* Hamburg: Hoffman und Campe.

Aybek, C. M. 2008. "Jugendliche aus Zuwandererfamilien im Übergang von der Schule in den Beruf—Perspektiven der Lebenslauf- und Integrationsforschung." In *Migrations- und Integrationsprozesse in Europa,* edited by U. Hunger, C. M. Aybek, A. Ette, and I. Michalowski. Wiesbaden: VS Verlag für Sozialwissenschaften.

Baethge, M. 2010. "Das deutsche Bildungs-Schisma: Welche Probleme ein vorindustrielles Bildungssystem in einer nachindustriellen Gesellschaft hat." *SOFI-Mitteilungen* 34:13–27.

Bartsch, Tillman, Barbara Bergmann, Wolfgang Stelly, Joerg Kinzig, Abdelmalek Hibaoui, Bernadette Schaffer, and Katharina Stengel. 2018. "Muslime im baden-wuerttembergsichen Justizvollzug." *Forum Strafvollzug* 1:52–57.

Batchelder, Lily. 2007. "Taxing Privilege More Effectively: Replacing the Estate Tax with an Inheritance Tax." Hamilton Project Discussion Paper, Brookings Institution, Washington, DC, June 2007.

Barry, Brian. 2002. *Culture and Equality.* Cambridge, MA: Harvard University Press.

Blau, Peter M. 1986. *Exchange and Power in Social Life.* Piscataway: Transaction.

Bobo, Lawrence D. 2012. "An American Conundrum: Race, Sociology, and the African American Road to Citizenship." In *The Oxford Handbook of African American Citizenship, 1865–Present,* edited by Lawrence D. Bobo, Lisa Crooms-Robinson, Linda Darling-Hammond, Michael C. Dawson, Henry Louis Gates Jr., Gerald Jaynes, and Claude Steele. New York: Oxford University Press.

Bold, Heike. 2020. *Inklusion an Grundschulen in Baden-Württemberg: Kompetenzen von Grundschullehrkraeften in der Kooperation mit sonderpädagogischen Lehrkräften.* Marburg: Tectum Wissenschaftsverlag.

Bonnet, Francois. 2019. *The Upper Limit: How Low Wage Work Defines Punishment and Welfare.* Oakland: University of California Press.

Bonnett, Alistair. 1998. "Who Was White? The Disappearance of Non-European White Identities and the Formation of European Racial Whiteness." *Ethnic and Racial Studies* 21, no. 6: 1029–55.

Bourgois, Philippe. 2002. *In Search of Respect: Selling Crack in El Barrio.* Cambridge: Cambridge University Press.

Bronson, Jennifer, and Marcus Berzofsky. 2017. "Indicators of Mental Health Problems Reported by Prisoners and Jail Inmates, 2011–2012." Special Report, US Department of Justice, June. https://bjs.ojp.gov/content/pub/pdf/imhprpji1112.pdf.

Browning, Christopher. 1992. *Ordinary Men Ordinary Men: Reserve Police Battalion 101 and the Final Solution in Poland.* New York: Harper.

Brubaker, Rogers. 1992. *Citizenship and Nationhood in France and Germany.* Cambridge, MA: Harvard University Press.

Bucerius, Sandra. 2014. *Unwanted: Muslim Immigrants, Dignity and Drug Dealing.* New York: Oxford University Press.

Burdick-Will, Julia. 2016. "Neighborhood Violent Crime and Academic Growth in Chicago: Lasting Effects of Early Exposure." *Social Forces* 95, no. 1: 133–58. https://doi.org/10.1093/sf/sow041.

Butterfield, Fox. 2018. *In My Father's House: A New View of How Crime Runs in the Family.* New York: Alfred A. Knopf.

Carson, Anne. 2020. *Prisoners in 2019.* NCJ 255115. Washington, DC: US Department of Justice, Office of Justice Programs, Bureau of Justice Statistics.

Chetty, Raj, John N. Friedman, Emmanuel Saez, Nichola Turner, and Danny Yagan. 2020. "Income Segregation and Intergenerational Mobility across Colleges in the United States." *Quarterly Journal of Economics* 135, no. 3: 1567–1633.

Ciaian, Pavel, and D'artis Kancs. 2018. "Social Mobility Barriers for Roma: Discrimination and Informal Institutions." *European Review* 26, no. 4: 670–85.

Coates, Ta-Nehishi. 2015. *Between the World and Me.* New York: Spiegel and Grau.

Cohen, Albert K. 1955. *Delinquent Boys: The Culture of the Gang.* New York: Free Press.

Confair, Amy, Amy Carroll-Scott, K. Castro, Y. Zhao, S. Melly, J. Kolker, S. Lankenau, and A. Roth. 2019. "Community Health Profile: Kensington, Philadelphia." Drexel University Urban Health Collaborative, Philadelphia, PA, October.

Contreras, Randol. 2013. *The Stickup Kids: Race, Drugs, Violence, and the American Dream.* Berkeley: University of California Press.

Cox, Alexandra. 2018. *Trapped in a Vice. The Consequences of Confinement for Young People.* New Brunswick, NJ: Rutgers University Press.

Crewe, Ben. 2009. *The Prisoner Society: Power, Adaptation and Social Life in an English Prison.* Oxford: Oxford University Press.

Cross, Linda, and William E. Cross Jr. 2005. "Transacting Black Identity: A Two-Week Daily-Diary Study." In *Navigating the Future: Social Identity, Coping, and Life Tasks,* edited by Geraldine Downey, Jacquelynne S. Eccles, Celina M. Chatman, 67–95. New York: Russell Sage Foundation.

Cross, William E. 1991. *Shades of Black.* Philadelphia: Temple University Press.

Dalton, Conley. 1999. *Being Black, Living in the Red. Race, Wealth, and Social Policy in America.* Berkeley: University of California Press.

Davis, Angela Y. 2003. *Are Prisons Obsolete?* New York: Seven Stories Press.

DeFina, Robert, and Lance Hannon. 2013. "The Impact of Mass Incarceration on Poverty." *Crime and Delinquency* 59, no. 4 (June): 562–86.

Diehl, Claudia, and Nadia Granto. 2018. "Germany: Intergenerational Inequalities in the Education System and the Labour Market for Native-Born Children of Immigrants from Turkey and the Former Yugoslavia." In *Catching Up? Country Studies on Intergenerational Mobility and Children of Immigrants.* Paris: OECD.

Dilulio, John. 1995. "The Coming of the Superpredators." *Weekly Standard,* November 27, 1995.

Du Bois, W. E. B. 1994. *The Souls of Black Folk.* New York: Dover.

Durkheim, Emile. 1960. *The Division of Labor In Society.* New York: Free Press.

Edin, Kathryn, and Luke H. Shaefer. 2015. *$2 A Day: Living on Almost Nothing in America.* New York: Houghton Mifflin Harcourt.

Ehrenreich, Barbara. 2001. *Nickel and Dimed: On (Not) Getting by in America.* New York: Metropolitan Books.

Elon, Amos. 2003. *The Pity of It All: A Portrait of Jews In Germany, 1743–1933.* New York: Picador.

Erikson, Kai T. 1966. *Wayward Puritans: A Study in the Sociology of Deviance.* Boston: Allyn & Bacon.

Esping-Andersen, Gøsta. 1990. "The Three Political Economies of the Welfare State." *International Journal of Sociology* 20, no. 3: 92–123.

Evans, Richard J. 1997. *Rituals of Retribution: Capital Punishment in Germany, 1600–1987.* Oxford: Oxford University Press.

Fader, Jamie. 2013. *Falling Back: Incarceration and Transitions to Adulthood among Urban Youth.* New Brunswick, NJ: Rutgers University Press.

Fair, Helen, and Roy Walmsley. 2021. *World Prison Population List.* 13th ed. London: Institute for Crime & Justice Policy Research. https://www.prisonstudies.org/sites/default/files/resources/downloads/world_prison_population_list_13th_edition.pdf.

Foucault, Michel. 1995. *Discipline and Punish: The Birth of the Prison.* New York: Vintage.

Frei, Norbert, ed. 2003. *Hitlers Eliten nach 1945.* Munich: dtv.

Fritz, Joachim, Britta Luettke, and Matthias Wolff. 2020. *Migrationshintergrund—Einführung eines Hochrechnungsverfahrens zum Ausgleich von Antwortausfaellen.* Nuremberg: Bundesagentur für Arbeit.

Garland, David. 2002. *The Culture of Control: Crime and Social Order in Contemporary Society.* Chicago: University of Chicago Press.

Gaventa, John. 1982. *Power and Powerlessness: Quiescence and Rebellion in an Appalachian Valley.* Chicago: University of Illinois Press.

Geertz, Clifford. 2017. *The Interpretation of Cultures.* New York: Basic Books.

Gil-Hernandez, Carlos J. 2019. "Do Well-Off Families Compensate for Low Cognitive Ability? Evidence on Social Inequality in Early Schooling from a Twin Study." *Sociology of Education* 92, no. 2: 150–75.

Gimple, James G. 1999. *Separate Destinations: Migration, Immigration, and the Politics of Places.* Ann Arbor: University of Michigan Press.

Goffman, Alice. 2014. *On the Run: Fugitive Life in an American City.* Chicago: University of Chicago Press.

Goldrick-Rab, S. 2010. "Challenges and Opportunities for Improving Community College Student Success." *Review of Educational Research* 80, no. 3: 437–69.

Gonzales, Roberto G. 2015. *Lives in Limbo: Undocumented and Coming of Age in America.* Berkeley: University of California Press.

Gumbel, Emil Julius. 2012. *Vier Jahre Politischer Mord.* Neuilly sur Seine: Ulan Press.

Haasler, Simone R. 2020. "The German System of Vocational Education and Training: Challenges of Gender, Academisation and the Integration of Low-Achieving Youth." *Transfer: European Review of Labour and Research* 26, no. 1 (February): 57–71. https://doi.org/10.1177/1024258919898115.

Habermas, Jürgen. 1985. *The Theory of Communicative Action.* Vol. 2, *Lifeworld and System: A Critique of Functionalist Reason.* New York: Beacon Press.

Hamilton, Darrick, and William Darity. 2010. "Can 'Baby Bonds' Eliminate the Racial Wealth Gap in Putative Post-racial America?" *Review of Black Political Economy* 37, no. 3–4 (January): 207–16.

Hamilton, Leah, Stephen Roll, Mathieu Despard, Elaine Maag, and Yung Chun. 2021. "Employment, Financial and Well-Being Effects of the 2021 Expanded Child Tax Credit." September 2021. St. Louis: Washington University in St. Louis, Social Policy Institute. https://cpb-us-w2.wpmucdn.com/sites.wustl.edu/dist/a/2003/files/2021/09/Wave-1-executive-summary_FINAL.pdf.

Haney, Lynne. 2010. *Offending Women: Power, Punishment, and the Regulation of Desire.* Berkeley: University of California Press.

Hanson, Rebecca, and Patricia Richards. 2019. *Harassed: Gender, Bodies, and Ethnographic Research.* Oakland: University of California Press.

Harding, David J. 2010. *Living the Drama: Community, Conflict, and Culture among Inner-City Boys.* Chicago: University of Chicago Press.

Hartmann, Christian. 2004. "Verbrecherischer Krieg- verbrecherische Wehrmacht. Überlegungen zur Struktur des Ostheeres, 1941–1944." *Vierteljahreshefte für Zeitgeschichte* 52, no. 1: 1–75.

Harlow, Caroline Wolf. 2003. *Education and Correctional Populations.* Bureau of Justice Statistics. Special Report. NCJ-195670. January 2003. https://bjs.ojp.gov/content/pub/pdf/ecp.pdf.

Haskins, Anna R. 2017. "Paternal Incarceration and Children's Schooling Contexts: Intersecting Inequalities of Educational Opportunity." *Annals of the American Academy of Political and Social Science* 674, no. 1: 134–62.

Hilberg, Raul. 1999. *Die Vernichtung der europäischen Juden.* 3 vols. Frankfurt: Fischer.

Hinton, Elizabeth. 2017. *From the War on Poverty to the War on Crime.* Cambridge, MA: Harvard University Press.

Hirschfeld, Paul J. 2018. "Schools and Crime." *Annual Review of Criminology* 1, no. 1: 149–69.

Hochmuth, Brigitte, Britta Kohlbrecher, Christian Merkl, and Hermann Gartner. 2019. "Hartz IV and the Decline of German Unemployment: A Macroeconomic Evaluation." IZA Discussion Paper Series 12260: 1–48.

Hochschild, Arlie Russell. 1989. *The Second Shift: Working Families and the Revolution at Home.* New York: Viking.

Hoffmann, Annette. 2018. *"Ein Versuch nur—immerhin ein Versuch": Die Zentrale Stelle in Ludwigsburg unter der Leitung von Erwin Schüle und Adalbert Rückerl (1958–1984).* Berlin: Metropol Verlag.

Hölzl, Martin. 2001. "Grüner Rock und weiße Weste: Adolf von Bomhard und die Legende von der sauberen Ordnungspolizei." *Zeitschrift für Geschichtswissenschaft* 50:22–43.

———. 2019. "Gutachten 'NS-Vergangenheit ehemaliger Behördenleiter des Landeskriminalamtes NRW.'" Polizei Nordrhein-Westfalen. Accessed April 28, 2023. https://lka.polizei.nrw/sites/default/files/2019-12/191211_Gutachten%20lang.pdf.

Höynck, Theresia, and Stephanie Ernst. 2014. "Jugendstrafrecht: Ein Vierteljahrhundert—schlechte Zeiten für rationale Kriminalpolitik." *Kritische Justiz* 47, no. 3: 249–60.

Jacoby, Tamar. 2014. "Why Germany Is So Much Better at Training Its Workers." *Atlantic*, October 16, 2014. https://www.theatlantic.com/business/archive/2014/10/why-germany-is-so-much-better-at-training-its-workers/381550/.

Jaehner, Harald. 2019. *Wolfszeit: Deutschland und die Deutschen, 1945–1955.* Hamburg: Rowohlt Verlag.

Jerolmack, Colin, and Shamus Khan. 2014. "Talk Is Cheap: Ethnography and the Attitudinal Fallacy." *Sociological Methods & Research*, 43, no.2: 178–209. https://doi.org/10.1177/0049124114523396

Joppke, Christian. 1999. *Immigration and the Nation-State. The United States, Germany, and Great Britain*. Oxford: Oxford University Press

Karlauf, Thomas. 2019. *Stauffenberg: Porträt eines Attentäters*. Munich: Blessing.

Kemper, Thomas. 2015. *Bildungsdisparitäten von Schülern nach Staatsange-hörigkeit und Migrationshintergrund. Eine schulformspezifische Analyse anhand von Daten der amtlichen Schulstatistik*. Münster: Waxmann.

Kende, Anna, Márton Hadarics, Sára Bigazzi, Mihaela Boza, Jonas R. Kunst, Nóra Anna Lantos, Barbara Lášticová, Anca Minescu, Monica Pivetti, and Ana Urbiola. 2021. "The Last Acceptable Prejudice in Europe? Anti-Gypsyism as the Obstacle to Roma Inclusion." *Group Processes and Intergroup Relations* 24, no. 3: 388–410.

Khan, Shamus Rahman. 2011. *Privilege: The Making of an Adolescent Elite at St. Pauls*. Princeton, NJ: Princeton University Press.

Klee, Ernst. 2013. *Auschwitz—Täter, Gehilfen, Opfer und was aus ihnen wurde: Ein Personenlexikon*. Frankfurt: Fischer.

Koopmans, Ruud. 2010. "Trade-Offs between Equality and Difference: Immigrant Integration, Multiculturalism and the Welfare State in Cross-National Perspective." *Journal of Ethnic and Migration Studies* 36, no. 1: 1–26.

Korn, Salomon. 1999. *Geteilte Vergangenheit, Beiträge zur "deutsch-jüdischen" Gegenwart*. Berlin: Philo.

Korteweg, Anna C., and Gökçe Yurdakul. 2014. *The Headscarf Debates: Conflicts of National Belonging*. Stanford, CA: Stanford University Press.

Kracuer, Siegfried. 1984. *Von Caligari bis Hitler: Eine psychologische Geschichte des deutschen Films*. Frankfurt: Suhrkamp.

Kränzler, Sonja, and Colin Cramer. 2020. *Soziale Herkunft von Schülerin-nen und Schülern an Gemeinschaftsschulen: Ein Ergebnisbericht*. Tübingen: Universität Tübingen.

Lamont Michèle, Stefan Beljean, and Matthew Clair. 2014. "What Is Missing? Cultural Processes and Causal Pathways to Inequality." *Socio-economic Review* 12, no. 3: 573–608.

Lappi-Seppälä, Tapio. 2007. "Penal Policy in Scandinavia." *Crime and Justice* 36, no. 1: 217–95.

Laubenthal, Klaus. 2007. "Die Renaissance der Sicherungsverwahrung." *Zeitschrift für die Gesamte Strafrechtswissenschaft* 116, no. 3: 703–50.

Lee, Hedwig, and Christopher Wildeman. 2021. "Assessing Mass Incarceration's Effects on Families." *Science* 374, no. 6565: 277–81.

Leverentz, Andrea. 2020. "Beyond Neighborhoods: Activity Spaces of Returning Prisoners." *Social Problems* 67, no. 1: 150–70. https://doi.org/10.1093/socpro/spz005.

Lewicki, A. 2014. *Social Justice through Citizenship? The Politics of Muslim Integration in Germany and Great Britain.* London: Palgrave Macmillan.

Lewis, Oscar. 1975. *Five Families: Mexican Case Studies in the Culture of Poverty.* New York: Basic Books.

Light, Michael T., Michael Massoglia, and Ryan D. King. 2014. "Citizenship and Punishment: The Salience of National Membership in U.S. Criminal Courts." *American Sociological Review* 79, no. 5: 825–47.

Lizardo, Omar, and Dustin S. Stoltz. 2018. "Max Weber's Ideal versus Material Interest Distinction Revisited." *European Journal of Social Theory* 21, no. 1: 3–21. https://doi.org/10.1177/1368431017710906.

Lopez-Aguado, Patrick. 2018. *Stick Together and Come Back Home: Racial Sorting and the Spillover of Carceral Identity.* Oakland: University of California Press.

Maaz, Kai, Jürgen Baumert, and Ulrich Trautwein. 2010. "Genese sozialer Ungleichheit im institutionellen Kontext der Schule: Wo entsteht und vergrößert sich soziale Ungleichheit?" In *Bildungsentscheidungen*, edited by Jürgen Baumert, Kai Maaz, and Ulrich Trautwein. Wiesbaden: VS Verlag für Sozialwissenschaften.

Mack, Julian W. 1909. "The Juvenile Court." *Harvard Law Review* 23, no. 2: 104–22. https://doi.org/10.2307/1325042.

MacLeod, Jay. 1987. *Ain't No Makin' It: Leveled Aspirations in a Low-Income Neighborhood.* Boulder, CO: Westview.

Marshall, Thomas H., and Tom Bottomore. 1992. *Citizenship and Social Class.* London: Pluto Press.

Massey, Douglas S. 2020. "Still the Linchpin: Segregation and Stratification in the USA." *Race and Social Problems* 12:1–12. https://doi.org/10.1007/s12552-019-09280-1.

Massey, Douglas, and Nancy Denton. 1994. *American Apartheid: Segregation and the Making of the Underclass.* Cambridge, MA: Harvard University Press.

McCaul, Edward J., Gordon A. Donaldson, Theodore Coladarci, and William E. Davis. 1992. "Consequences of Dropping Out of School: Findings from High School and Beyond." *Journal of Educational Research* 85, no. 4: 198–207. http://www.jstor.org/stable/27540476.

McFarland, Joel, Jiashan Cui, Amy Rathbun, and Juliet Holmes. 2019. "Trends in High School Dropout and Completion Rates in the United States: 2019." Washington, DC: US Department of Education. https://nces.ed.gov/pubs2019/2019117.pdf.

McGarry, Aidan. 2014. "Roma as a Political Identity: Exploring Representations of Roma in Europe." *Ethnicities* 14, no. 6: 756–74.

Mead, George Herbert. 1918. "The Psychology of Punitive Justice." *American Journal of Sociology* 23, no. 5: 577–602.

———. 1967. *Mind, Self, and Society: From the Standpoint of a Social Behaviorist.* Chicago: University of Chicago Press.

Merton, Robert K. 1938. "Social Structure and Anomie." *American Sociological Review* 3, no. 5: 672–82.

Messner, Steven F., and Richard Rosenfeld. 2007. *Crime and the American Dream.* Belmont, CA: Wadsworth.

Mommsen, Hans. 1991. *From Weimar to Auschwitz: Essays in German History.* London: Polity Press.

Morris, Edward W., and Brea L. Perry. 2016. "The Punishment Gap: School Suspension and Racial Disparities in Achievement." *Social Problems* 6, no.1 (2016): 68–86. https://doi.org/10.1093/socpro/spv026.

Muller, Christopher, and Alexander F. Roehrkasse. 2022. "Racial and Class Inequality in US Incarceration in the Early Twenty-First Century." *Social Forces* 101, no. 2: 803–28. https://doi.org/10.1093/sf/soab141.

Münzenmaier, Werner. 2020. "Geldvermögen und Einkommen in den Kreisen des Landes Baden-Württemberg." Baden-Württemberg: Statistisches Landesamt. Accessed April 28, 2023. https://www.statistik-bw.de/Service/Veroeff/Monatshefte/20200504?path=/PrivHaushalte/AusstattVermoegen/.

Myrdal, Gunnar. 1995. *An American Dilemma: The Negro Problem and Modern Democracy*. Vol. 1. New York: Routledge.

Narimani, Petra. 2017. "Frei und doch in Haft: Drogenkonsum und Aufenthaltsstatus." PhD diss., Freie Universität Berlin.

Ochel, Wolfgang. 2005. *Welfare to Work in Germany*. CESifo DICE Report. February 2005. https://www.ifo.de/DocDL/dicereport205 -forum4.pdf.

Odendahl, Christian. 2017. "The Hartz Myth: A Closer Look at Germany's Labour Market Reforms." Center for European Reform. July 10, 2017. https://www.cer.eu/sites/default/files/pbrief_german _labour_19.7.17.pdf.

Oers, Ricky van. 2021. "Deserving Citizenship in Germany and The Netherlands: Citizenship Tests in Liberal Democracies." *Ethnicities* 21, no. 2 (April): 271–88.

The Opioid Threat in Pennsylvania. 2018. DEA Philadelphia Division and the University of Pittsburgh. September. https://www.dea.gov/ sites/default/files/2018-10/PA%20Opioid%20Report%20Final %20FINAL.pdf.

Owens, Ann. 2020. "Unequal Opportunity: School and Neighborhood Segregation in the USA." *Race and Social Problems* 12, no. 1: 29–41.

Pager, Devah. 2003. "The Mark of a Criminal Record." *American Journal of Sociology* 108, no. 5: 937–75.

Panreck, Isabelle-Christine, and Heinz Ulrich Brinkmann. 2019. "Migration und Rechtspopulismus—zwei Seiten einer Medaille?" In *Rechtspopulismus in Einwanderungsgesellschaften*, edited by Heinz Ulrich Brinkmann and Isabelle-Christine Panreck. Wiesbaden: Springer. https://doi.org/10.1007/978-3-658-2-3401-0_1.

Partridge, Damani J. 2012. *Hypersexuality and Headscarves: Race, Sex, and Citizenship in the New Germany*. Bloomington: Indiana University Press, 2012.

Patterson, Orlando. 1982. *Slavery and Social Death: A Comparative Study*. Cambridge, MA: Harvard University Press.

Pattillo, Mary. 1999. *Black Picket Fences: Privilege and Peril among the Black Middle Class*. Chicago: University of Chicago Press.

Pelletier, Elizabeth, and Paul Manna. 2017. "Learning in Harm's Way: Neighborhood Violence, Inequality, and American Schools." *Annals of the American Academy of Political and Social Science* 674, no. 1: 217–39.

Pendas, Devin O. 2010. *The Frankfurt Auschwitz Trial, 1963–1965: Genocide, History and the Limits of the Law.* Cambridge: Cambridge University Press.

Perels, Joachim. 2004. "Die Übernahme der Beamtenschaft des Hitler-Regimes: Benachteiligung Der Entlassenen Und Privilegierung Der Amtsinhaber Der Diktatur." *Kritische Justiz* 37, no. 2: 186–93. http://www.jstor.org/stable/24237816.

Pew Research Center. 2018. "Shifting Public Views on Legal Immigration into the U.S." Pew Research Center. June 28, 2018. https://www.pewresearch.org/politics/2018/06/28/shifting-public-views-on-legal-immigration-into-the-u-s/.

Pfaff, John. 2017. *Locked In: The True Causes of Mass Incarceration—And How to Achieve Real Reform.* New York: Basic Books.

Phelps, Michelle. 2011. "Rehabilitation in the Punitive Era: The Gap between Rhetoric and Reality in U.S. Prison Programs." *Law and Society Review* 45, no. 1: 33–68.

Piven, Frances Fox, and Richard A. Cloward. 1993. *Regulating the Poor: The Function of Public Welfare.* New York: Vintage.

Plamper, Jan. 2019. *Das neue Wir: Warum Migration dazugehört; Eine andere Geschichte der Deutschen.* Frankfurt: S. Fischer.

Platt, Anthony M. 1977. *The Child Savers: The Invention of Delinquency.* Chicago: University of Chicago Press.

Plessner, Helmuth. 2001. *Die verspätete Nation: über die politische Verführbarkeit bürgerlichen Geistes.* Frankfurt: Suhrkamp.

Poole, Mary Kathryn, Sheila E. Fleischhacker, and Sara N. Bleich. 2021. "Addressing Child Hunger When School Is Closed—Considerations during the Pandemic and Beyond." *New England Journal of Medicine* 384, no. 10: e35.

Prasad, Monica. 2012. *The Land of Too Much: American Abundance and the Paradox of Poverty.* Cambridge, MA: Harvard University Press.

Prins, Seth J. 2014. "The Prevalence of Mental Illness in U.S State Prisons: A Systematic Review." *Psychiatric Services* 65:862–72.

Ragin, Charles C., and Howard Saul Becker. 1992. *What Is a Case? Exploring the Foundations of Social Inquiry.* Cambridge: Cambridge University Press.

Raudenbush, Steven, and Robert D. Eschmann. 2015. "Does Schooling Increase or Reduce Social Inequality." *Annual Review of Sociology* 41:443–70.

Reed, Adolph. 2020. "Socialism and the Argument against Race Reductionism." *New Labor Forum* 29, no. 2: 36–43.

Reeves, Richard V. 2017. *Dream Hoarders: How the American Upper Middle Class is Leaving Everyone Else in the Dust, Why That Is a Problem, and What to Do About It.* Washington, DC: Brookings Institution Press.

Rigoll, Dominik. 2017. *Staatsschutz in Westdeutschland: Von der Entnazifizierung zur Extremistenabwehr.* Göttingen: Wallstein Verlag.

Rios, Victor M. 2011. *Punished: Policing the Lives of Black and Latino Boys.* New York: NYU Press.

Roberts, Jennifer, and Julie Horney. 2010. "The Life Event Calendar Method in Criminological Research." In *Handbook of Quantitative Criminology*, edited by Alex Piquero and David Weisburd. New York: Springer.

Rothman, David J. 2008. *The Discovery of the Asylum. Social Order and Disorder in the New Republic.* New Brunswick, NJ: Aldine Transactions.

Rubin, Ashley T. 2021. *The Deviant Prison: Philadelphia's Eastern State Penitentiary and the Origins of Americas Penal System 1829–1913.* Cambridge: Cambridge University Press.

Rucht, Dieter, and Mundo Yang. 2004. "Wer demonstriert gegen Hartz IV." *Forschungsjournal Soziale Bewebung* 17, no. 4: 21–27.

Rudes, Danielle S., Shannon Magnuson, and Angela Hattery. 2022. *Surviving Solitary: Living and Working in Restricted Housing Units.* Stanford, CA: Stanford University Press.

Rusche, Georg, and Otto Kirchheimer. 2003. *Punishment and Social Structure.* London: Routledge.

Sassen, Saskia. 2001. *The Global City: New York, London, Tokyo.* Princeton, NJ: Princeton University Press

Satter, Berry. 2009. *Family Properties: How the Struggle over Race and Real Estate Transformed Chicago and Urban America.* New York: Picador.

Savelsberg, Joachim. 1994. "Knowledge, Domination, and Criminal Punishment." *American Journal of Sociology* 99, no. 4: 911–43.

Schiller, Kay. 2015. "'Siegen für Deutschland?' Patriotism, Nationalism and the German National Football Team, 1954–2014." *Historische Sozialforschung* 40, no. 4 (154): 176–96.

Schneider, Jens. 2018. "'Ausländer' (Foreigners), Migrants, or New Germans? Identity-Building Processes and School Socialization among Adolescents from Immigrant Backgrounds in Germany." In "Navigating Pathways in Multicultural Nations: Identities, Future Orientation, Schooling, and Careers," edited by Catherine R. Cooper and Rachel Seginer. Special issue, *New Directions for Child and Adolescent Development* 160: 59–73.

Schneider, Luisa. 2021. "Let Me Take a Vacation in Prison before the Streets Kill Me! Rough Sleepers' Longing for Prison and the Reversal of Less Eligibility in Neoliberal Carceral Continuums." *Punishment and Society* 25, no. 1. https://doi.org/10.1177/14624745211010222.

Sharkey, Patrick. 2013. *Stuck in Place: Urban Neighborhoods and the End of Progress toward Racial Equality.* Chicago: University of Chicago Press.

Shedd, Carla. 2015. *Unequal City: Race, Schools and Perceptions of Injustice.* New York: Russell Sage.

Simmel, Georg. 1971. "The Stranger." In *Individuality and Social Forms*, edited by Donald N. Levine, 143–49. Chicago: University of Chicago Press.

Skiba, Russell J., Robert. H. Horner, Chon-Geun. Chung, M. Karega Rausch, Seth. L. May, and Tary Tobin. 2019. "Race Is Not Neutral: A National Investigation of African American and Latino Disproportionality in School Discipline." *School Psychology Review* 40, no. 1: 85–107.

Slavinski, Ilya, and Kimberly Spencer-Suarez. 2021. "The Price of Poverty: Policy Implications of the Unequal Effects of Monetary Sanctions on the Poor." *Journal of Contemporary Criminal Justice* 37, no. 1: 45–65. https://doi.org/10.1177/1043986220971395.

Small, Mario L. 2004. *Villa Victoria: The Transformation of Social Capital in a Boston Barrio.* Chicago: University of Chicago Press.

———. 2017. *Someone to Talk To.* New York: Oxford University Press

Small, Mario Luis, David J. Harding, and Michèle Lamont. 2010. "Reconsidering Culture and Poverty." *Annals of the American Academy of Political and Social Science* 629, no. 1: 6–27.

Solms, Wilgheim. 2008. *Zigeunerbilder. Ein dunkles Kapitel der deutschen Literaturgeschichte. Von der frühen Neuzeit bis zur Romantik*. Würzburg: Königshausen u. Neumann.

Soss, Joe, Richard C. Fording, and Sanford F. Schram. 2011. *Disciplining the Poor: Neoliberal Paternalism and the Persistent Power of Race*. Chicago: University of Chicago Press.

Soyer, Michaela. 2016. *A Dream Denied: Incarceration, Recidivism and Young Minority Men*. Oakland: University of California Press.

———. 2018. *Lost Childhoods: Poverty, Trauma and Violent Crime in the Post-Welfare Era*. Oakland: University of California Press.

Spindler, Susanne. 2011. "Wer hat Angst vor Mehmet? Medien, Politik und die Kriminalisierung von Migration." In *Die Vermessung der sozialen Welt*, edited by G. Hentges and B. Lösch. Hamburg: VS Verlag für Sozialwissenschaften. https://doi.org/10.1007/978-3-531-92756-5_21.

Steele, Claude M., and Joshua Aronson. 1995. "Stereotype Threat and the Intellectual Test Performance of African Americans." *Journal of Personality and Social Psychology* 69, no. 5: 797–811.

Steinberg, Jonathan. 2011. *Bismarck: A Life*. Oxford: Oxford University Press.

Stelly, W., and J. Thomas. 2015. *Evaluation des Jugendstrafvollzuge in Baden-Württemberg*. Stuttgart: Kriminologischer Dienst Baden-Württemberg.

———. 2017. *Evaluation des Jugendstrafvollzuge in Baden-Württemberg*. Stuttgart: Kriminologischer Dienst Baden-Württemberg.

———. 2021. *Evaluation des Jugendstrafvollzuge in Baden-Württemberg*. Stuttgart: Kriminologischer Dienst Baden-Württemberg. (These are different reports for three different years.)

Stern, Fritz, 1977. *Gold and Iron: Bismarck, Bleichröder and the Building of the German Empire*. New York: Alfred A. Knopf.

Stone, Lewi. 2019. "Quantifying the Holocaust: Hyperintense Kill Rates during the Nazi Genocide." *Science Advances* 5, no 1. https://doi.org/10.1126/sciadv.aau7292.

Strothmann, Dietrich. 1964. "Hinter verhangenen Fenstern: Ein Tag im Auschwitz Prozess." *Die Zeit*, January 31, 1964. https://www.zeit.de/1964/05/index?wt_zmc=fix.int.zonpme.zeitde.wall_abo

.premium.packshot.cover.zear&utm_medium=fix&utm_source
=zeitde_zonpme_int&utm_campaign=wall_abo&utm_content
=premium_packshot_cover_zear.

Sufrin, Carolyn. 2017. *Jailcare: Finding the Safety Net for Women behind Bars*. Oakland: University of California Press.

Sun, Sicong, Jin Huang, Darrell L. Hudson, and Michael Sherraden. 2021. "Cash Transfers and Health." *Annual Review of Public Health* 42:363–80.

Swidler, Ann. 1986. "Culture in Action: Symbols and Strategies." *American Sociological Review* 51, no. 2: 273–86.

Teplin, Linda A., Karen M. Abram, Gary M. McClelland, Mina K. Dulcan, and Amy A. Mericle. 2003. "Psychiatric Disorders in Youth in Juvenile Detention." *Archives of General Psychiatry* 59:1133–43.

Tönnies, Ferdinand. 1957. *Community and Society*. East Lansing: Michigan State University Press.

Tran, Van C. 2016. "Ethnic Culture and Social Mobility among the Asian Second Generation." *Ethnic and Racial Studies* 39, no. 13: 2398–403.

Tuchel, Johannes. 2019. *Hinrichtungen im Strafgefängnis Berlin-Plötzensee 1933 bis 1945*. Berlin: Gedenkstätte Deutscher Widerstand.

Valle, Ariana J. 2019. "Race and the Empire-State: Puerto Ricans' Unequal U.S. Citizenship." *Sociology of Race and Ethnicity* 5, no. 1: 26–40.

Van Cleve Gonzales, Nicole. 2016. *Crook County: Racism and Injustice in America's Largest Criminal Court*. Stanford, CA: Stanford University Press.

Venkatesh, Sudhir Alladi. 2002. *American Project: The Rise and Fall of a Modern Ghetto*. Cambridge, MA: Harvard University Press.

Wacquant, Loïc. 2005. "Carnal Connections: On Embodiment, Apprenticeship and Membership." *Qualitative Sociology* 28, no. 4: 445–74.

———. 2009. *Punishing the Poor: The Neoliberal Governmentality of Social Inequality*. Durham, NC: Duke University Press.

Wakefield, Sara, and Christopher Wildeman. 2013. *Children of the Prison Boom: Mass Incarceration and the Future of American Inequality*. New York: Oxford University Press.

Walter, Joachim. 2003. "Entwicklungen und Herausforderungen im deutschen Jugendstrafvollzug." *Neue Kriminalpolitk* 16, no. 1: 10–14.

Walton, Gregory M., Steven J. Spencer, and Sam Erman. 2013. "Affirmative Meritocracy." *Social Issues and Policy Review* 7, no. 1: 1–35.

Weber, Max. 1949. *Methodology and the Social Sciences.* Edited and translated by Edward A. Shils and Henry A. Finch. Glencoe, IL: Free Press.

———. 1958. *From Max Weber: Essays in Sociology.* Edited and translated by Hans H. Gerth and Wright Mills. New York: Oxford University Press.

———. 1978. *Economy and Society.* Berkeley: University of California Press.

Wegmann, Kate M., and Brittani Smith. 2019. "Examining Racial/Ethnic Disparities in School Discipline in the Context of Student-Reported Behavior Infractions." *Children and Youth Services Review* 103:18–27.

Welzer, Harald. 2002. *Opa war kein Nazi: Nationalsozialismus und Holocaust im Familiengedächtnis.* Frankfurt: Fischer.

Wenzel, Kirsten, and Silke Klewin. *Wege nach Bautzen II: Biographische und Autobiographische Porträts.* Dresden: Stiftung Sächsische Gedenkstätten zur Erinnerung an die Opfer politischer Gewaltherrschaft, 1998.

Wesner, Heike. 2018. "Land schwimmt mit einem Rekordüberschuss von 2,8 Milliarden weiter im Geld." *Pressmitteilung SPD Baden-Württemberg.* February 8. https://www.spd-landtag-bw.de/land-schwimmt-mit-einem-rekordueberschuss-von-28-milliarden-weiter-im-geld/.

Western, Bruce. 2006. *Punishment and Inequality in America.* New York: Russell Sage Foundation.

Western, Bruce, Anthony Braga, Jaclyn Davis, and Catherine Sirois. 2015. "Stress and Hardship after Prison." *American Journal of Sociology* 120, no. 5: 1512–47.

Western, Bruce, and Becky Pettit. 2010. "Incarceration and Social Inequality." *Daedalus* 139, no. 3: 8–19. https://doi.org/10.1162/daed_a_00019.

Wetzel, Maria. 2018. "Spendabel." *Stuttgarter Zeitung.* October 23, 2018. https://www.stuttgarter-zeitung.de/inhalt.kabinett-beschliesst-nachtragshaushalt-spendabel.fac26e91-9811-4388-a563-cf7c3fa99d19.html.

Whitman, James Q. 2005. *Harsh Justice: Criminal Punishment and the Widening Divide between America and Europe.* New York: Oxford University Press.

Williams, Helen. 2014. "Changing the National Narrative: Evolution in Citizenship and Integration in Germany, 2000–10." *Journal of Contemporary History* 49, no. 1: 54–74. https://doi.org/10.1177/002200 9413505658.

Willis, Paul. 1977. *Learning to Labor: How Working-Class Kids Get Working-Class Jobs.* New York: Columbia University Press.

Wilson, William Julius. 1990. *The Truly Disadvantaged: The Inner City, the Underclass, and Public Policy.* Chicago: University of Chicago Press.

Young, Alford A. 2004. *The Minds of Marginalized Black Men: Making Sense of Mobility, Opportunity, and Future Life Chances.* Princeton, NJ: Princeton University Press.

Yurdakul, Gökçe, and Anna C. Korteweg. 2013. "Gender Equality and Immigrant Integration: Honor Killing and Forced Marriage Debates in the Netherlands, Germany, and Britain." *Women's Studies International Forum* 41, no. 3: 204–14.

Zimring, Franklin E. 2005. *American Juvenile Justice.* Oxford: Oxford University Press.

INDEX